New Ideas in
Flower
Gardening

by
Derek Fell

Featured on the Covers —
Front Cover: Colorful annuals in containers bring "instant beauty" to
a vacation home; Rose "Miss All-America Beauty"; Daffodil mixture;
Tree peony "Hakuo-Jishi"; Caspian Lotus; Marigold "Jubilee".
Back Cover: Salvia "Evening Glow".

Art by Heather O'Connor

Countryside
Books

Copyright© 1976 by Countryside Books
A.B. Morse Company, 200 James Street, Barrington, IL 60010
Second printing, September, 1977

Printed in U.S.A.

Derek Fell, the author, examines a new hybrid trumpet lily during a recent visit to Japan.

magazines, and he is a contributor to *Encyclopaedia Britannica.* He is also a member of the Garden Writers Association of America and editor of the *Garden Writers Bulletin.*

For nearly three years Derek Fell worked as director of both the National Garden Bureau (an information office sponsored by the seed industry) and All-America Selections (the national seed trials). His news sheets for the National Garden Bureau were distributed to more than 5,000 news media including newspapers, magazines, television and radio. His press releases for All-America Selections reached an estimated audience of 62,000,000 people. This exposure and his work for the National Garden Bureau made him one of the most widely read garden writers in America.

He learned the art of plant photography from the late Harry Smith, England's finest plant photographer, and now maintains a color transparency library of more than 5,000 horticultural subjects, which is used extensively in his new capacity as a writer and consultant in the gardening field.

In recent years he has also traveled abroad seeking new flower varieties in Europe and the Orient. His first book, *How to Plant a Vegetable Garden*, was published by Countryside Books in March 1975.

About the Author

Derek Fell's enthusiasm for plants and gardens is reflected in some of the work he has conducted during the past fifteen years.

A transplanted Englishman, he began his writing career in England as a newspaper reporter and then became a public information specialist for horticultural products in London. He helped Jan de Graaff, the famous American lily hybridizer, introduce his hybrid lilies into Great Britain. He also worked for Europe's biggest wholesale seed house on the introduction of new flower seed varieties.

He moved to America to edit garden seed catalogs after winning all three awards in the wholesale section of Britain's Best Seed Catalog Contest — first overall best, first best selling and first best reference.

Over the past several years he has appeared on television talk shows discussing gardening from seed. He lectures and writes extensively for newspapers and

About the Photography

Most of the color photographs in this book were taken by the author over a period of eight years, using only natural light and photographing the plants exactly as they grew in natural surroundings. They were taken with a standard Rolleiflex camera on Ektachrome film. No tripods, artificial light, filters, lens shields, wind breaks, or camera accessories of any other kind were used.

The line etchings used throughout the book are taken from turn-of-the-century seed catalogs. This intricate engraving art unfortunately disappeared with the invention of the camera and the discovery among seedsmen that photographic illustrations sold far more of their product than line artwork.

Contents

Corner of rose garden overlooks a rock garden in foreground. Wall behind roses screens a sunbathing area of smooth white beach pebbles.

The Author's Garden

Shortly after we moved to the United States from England in 1967, my wife and I bought a house that could serve not only as a home, but also as a place to work. The property occupies two acres at the end of a long gravel driveway and slopes down to a quiet creek and a pond where snowy egrets, great blue herons, belted kingfishers and mallard ducks come to feed.

The house is contemporary in design, thrust into the hillside directly overlooking the pond. In the dining room a wall of plate glass separates the inside from the outside, but the indoors is so well landscaped with plants that it is difficult to tell where the outdoors ends and the indoors begins. A sunken garden runs almost the entire length of one dining room wall, constructed of rough stone. Baby's tears, a ground cover, hug the stones like moss, and bright red flowers of impatiens glare from the greenery. Towards the window, shade-loving plants give way to sun-loving kinds — aloes, crown of thorns, coleus, kalanchoes and geraniums. Hanging baskets complete the picture — graceful spider plants (*chlorophytum*) and variegated tradescantia.

The airy, peaked living room is alive with more plants. Over 100 varieties of desert cactus and succulents crowd a built-in planter and flower under huge picture windows. Two large jade plants are positioned at both ends, and in between grow stapelias, lithops, faucaria, bunny's ears (*opuntia microdasys*),

astrophytum and gasterias to mention only a few.

Outdoors there is a never-ending panorama of beauty, beginning in spring with magnificent specimens of *magnolia soulangeana*, forsythia, dogwoods, flowering cherries, ornamental crabapples, azaleas and rhododendrons. White wisteria, golden-yellow laburnum, pink smoke tree, viburnum and philadelphus continue the parade of beauty. Honeysuckle cascades down from the hedgerow and fills the air with its haunting fragrance, but the most vivid spectacle of all is the 80 foot rose hedge — in mid-June a solid stroke of shocking pink from the edge of the pond to the top of the lawn.

Sedum and prickly pear smother themselves with gorgeous flowers in a miniature rock garden adjoining a sun patio surfaced with smooth round beach pebbles and isolated from the world by a tiered ivy-covered wall.

Stategically placed containers cascade with petunias or erupt with begonias, French marigolds and other colorful annuals. On the far stream bank, clumps of yucca stab the sky with their white flower spikes.

In fall it is the trees that brighten the garden. Two ancient sassafras are the last to unfurl their leaves in spring and among the first to color in fall, presenting a display of color like a Van Gogh painting. Two mighty willows overhang the stream as it enters the property, while two more edge the pond — one a corkscrew with twisted branches that present a tortured silhouette in winter.

Evergreens, too, are in abundance. Favorites among them are the sturdy spruce, numerous pines that produce bushels of cones for decoration and mulch, and two splendid atlas cedars on the front lawn.

Several wild mulberry trees yield juicy fruit, and since they're all in the hedgerow, the falling fruit makes no mess at all. An apple and a pear have started to bear, but wine berries, wild strawberries and black raspberries also produce a bountiful harvest from the edges of the wild hedgerows.

Another delight is the "wild area" on the other side of the stream, accessible by an arched bridge. Here the deer come to munch wild apples, and the squirrels to nibble on wild Osage-orange fruits. Tall junipers stand so thick in this wild area that not a blade of grass grows beneath. In other places the brambles and vines are so dense barely a rabbit can pass through.

From the wild area, you can gain a good view of a heated indoor swimming pool which is home to a wide variety of indoor plants that thrive in the humid atmosphere and create a jungle effect along one wall.

Finally, there is the vegetable garden, located near the arched bridge and fenced in for protection from the deer, the rabbits, the muskrats and the ducks. It produces generous amounts of fresh vegetables from May until December.

These two acres contain just about everything a gardener could desire — a beautiful house, a lovely garden, stately trees, a stream, a pond, wild birds and friendly animals. A place to live; a place to work; and a place to garden.

The Value of Flower Gardens

The last miracle wrought by Napoleon, according to biographer Emile Ludwig, was a verdant garden created during his last years in exile on St. Helena — an inhospitable windswept volcanic island in the Atlantic. He made flowers bloom, vegetables grow and trees bear fruit where nothing but granite rock could endure the constant winds and depressing climate. Like other great leaders, Napoleon was fond of gardens, finding in them both privacy and inspiration to fuel his creative ideals.

The emperors of Japan and China recognized gardens as an art form, and at Kyoto, the ancient capital of imperial Japan, gardens survive today, exhibiting such artistic beauty that they dwarf all other treasures of the Orient.

Sir Joseph Banks, a wealthy 18th century British botanist, was fired with such enthusiasm for plants and gardens that he helped to finance the fantastic voyages of Captain James Cook. They turned into the greatest voyages of adventure and discovery ever made by man and began an era of pioneering and colonizing that has shaped the destiny of the world, and inspired an era of plant exploration that continues to this day.

The great Jewish banking family of Rothschilds and the famous American family of duPonts not only forged financial empires, but also found satisfaction in creating some of the most beautiful gardens of the world — at Exbury in England, at Winterthur in Delaware, and at Longwood Gardens in Pennsylvania.

At the grand palace of Versailles near Paris (France), Marie Antoinette created a cluster of cottage gardens called Le Petit Hameau to provide an escape from the formalities of court life. To many visitors, the magnificence and grandeur of Versailles pales in comparison to this little piece of heaven cherished by the last Queen of France.

Marie Antoinette, last Queen of France, inspired this cluster of quaint cottages and gardens called le Petit Hameau. Balconies cascading with geraniums, thatched cottages with "pocket-handkerchief" yards, a mill house, streams and bridges are grouped around a beautiful pond bordered with water lilies and willows.

Kew Gardens in England became the world's leading botanical garden under the directorship of Sir Joseph Banks, a wealthy botanist. He not only helped finance the amazing voyages of Captain James Cook to further exploration, but also was responsible for sending Captain William Bligh on the world's most sinister voyage of plant exploration — ending in the famous mutiny on the Bounty.

It is not within the means of everyone to afford the time and cost of gardens such as these, yet it is within the reach of many of us to improve our lives by seeking out the charm and serenity of small or public gardens.

A world without flowers would be a very sterile world indeed, and it is a comforting prospect to see that America is on the verge of becoming the greatest gardening nation in the world. For many American families until recently a garden has consisted of a large expanse of lawn and a few foundation plantings. But now Americans are turning to their homes and gardens for more pleasure. Driving the car long distances on weekends no longer has the mass appeal it used to have, and our gardens are taking on a new importance . . . a new value.

America is more fortunate than other great gardening nations — like Japan and Great Britain. Land there is at a premium, and for them the golden age of gardening has long since peaked. But in America we are at the beginning of a new age, where gardening and flower gardens seem destined to play a much greater part in our lives and our culture.

This book is neither an encyclopaedia nor a dictionary describing every conceivable variety of annual and perennial that can be grown in America. It is more a book of *ideas* — a selection of the best plants for beautifying our environment — and I apologize if I have left out anyone's favorite. Some flowers presented here are familiar, others unusual, but all are practical for the majority of American gardens, whether you have a small or large area, a sunny or shaded location, and whether you desire flowers for fragrance, cutting or pure ornamental display.

I hope overall I have transmitted my own feeling and appreciation for flowers — not a mass of varieties too numerous to digest, but a careful selection guaranteed to please, illustrated by realistic color pictures showing exactly how the plants can grow.

Taking Care of the Flower Bed

The foundation of a successful flower garden is the soil in which you expect plants to live, and the two most important physical characteristics of soil are good drainage and good *tilth* to a depth of at least one foot. By *tilth* we mean soil that has a crumbly texture in which roots can penetrate freely, drawing moisture and nutrients with ease. Clay soils and sandy soils do not have good tilth. Clay soils are too heavy, prone to waterlogging and excessive coldness. Wet and unworkable in winter, they bake rock-hard in summer. Sandy soils have no holding capacity, allowing moisture and nutrients to drain away too rapidly.

To improve a clay soil, you must break it up and add a soil conditioner. Bales of peat moss, garden compost, well-decomposed animal manures and leaf mold are excellent soil conditioners that can be used to improve both heavy clay soils and sandy soils.

Compost Heaps

Every garden benefits from a compost pile where kitchen wastes, grass clippings, shredded leaves, soft plant stems and animal manures are piled in a neat corner and allowed to decompose into a humus-rich, odorless, fine crumbly soil for adding to flower beds to improve soil texture. Don't rely on a compost pile to provide essential plant nutrients, however. Unless it is boxed to prevent leaching, and built up like a layer cake with nutrient-organic materials specially added, its main value will be as a soil conditioner — and not necessarily as a soil fertilizer.

Fertilizer

For successful results, all flowering plants need *moisture, sunlight* and *nutrients* in varying degrees.

The most important plant nutrients are *nitrogen, phosphorus* and *potash*. For leafy plants nitrogen is the most important ingredient, but for bulbous plants like iris, daffodils and dahlias, phosphorous is more important, stimulating underground root development.

All these nutrients can be added to the soil in organic form. For example, animal manures are high in nitrogen, bone meal is a good source of phosphorus, and wood ashes are a good source of potash. In addition to adding nutrients to the soil, they help to improve the soil texture.

These nutrients are also readily available in packaged form from nurseries, garden centers and hardware stores, mixed in exactly the right proportion for the job you want done — one kind for annual and perennial flowers, another for acid-loving plants like primulas and rhododendrons, and others specially formulated for bulbs and roses.

The easiest packaged fertilizer to use is *slow release,* or *timed-release,* fertilizer in dry granular form which can be sprinkled on the soil by hand at planting time. Read package instructions carefully, since some fertilizers that are not slow release need applying ten days *before* planting to prevent burning.

Foliar feeding is a technique whereby granules are mixed with water and applied to leaf surfaces with a spray or watering can for the plants to absorb nutrients through their leaves.

Weeds and Other Pests

Weeds can quickly smother flower beds if left uncontrolled, and a few minutes each day pulling a handful of weeds is far better than trying to catch up on two weeks of neglect. Also, there are packaged weed-killers, which can ease the problem of weeding, generally available in two forms — one to kill weed seeds before they germinate, and another to spot-kill weeds after they are established.

Obviously, a preventative weed-killer that kills weed seeds should be used directly on the soil only around established perennial shrub or tree plantings, and not on foliage, seed beds or around young delicate seedlings.

Spot weed-killers in jet-spray form destroy weeds that are already established. Care should be taken to aim well so as not to spray foliage of desirable plants.

Other common pests are insects and fungus diseases for which there are also effective packaged controls, such as vegetable dusts and pellets. The worst fungus diseases are *powdery mildew,* which shows itself as a powdery white coating on leaves and stems (especially zinnias), and *blackspot,* which causes ugly black blemishes and leaf drop (especially roses). *Aphids* and *spider mites* are tiny insect colonies which can cause heavy damage on roses and dahlias in particular. *Slugs* and *snails* have enormous appetites for leafy plants and will even strip marigolds down to the stem, but pellets sprinkled in among the flower beds will control them.

Mulching

Mulching is a good practice. Any decorative organic material spread on the ground around plants not only will control weeds, but also will help conserve moisture and maintain an even soil temperature. Grass clippings and leaves tend to make the soil too hot, but pine bark, pine needles, peat moss, straw, coco-beans and similar materials can be applied each spring to good effect.

Getting Plants for the Garden

Four main ways to add plants to your garden are by purchasing transplants and bulbs, starting seeds at home, and purchasing or starting rooted cuttings.

Transplants

The easiest, most foolproof method of adding flowering plants to your garden is by purchasing transplants, bedding plants or pot plants from a garden center or nursery. These can be had in a ready-to-bloom bud stage or in an advanced flowering stage. Larger perennials and flowering shrubs can be purchased in cans or large pots with sizeable root balls, so that transplanting disturbance is minimal. This is "instant gardening," and like other convenience products, you must pay extra for this convenience.

Just as there are good and poor quality seeds, it's possible to have good and poor quality transplants. Here are some ways to recognize a top quality transplant:

1 — Avoid long, lanky specimens that have had to stetch towards the light or have produced a spindly growth owing to overcrowding of roots. A dwarf, compact, bushy plant with some side shoots formed is better than a tall, thin, straggly specimen.

2 — Look for healthy dark green color in marigolds, salvias, petunias, impatiens and most other popular bedding plants. Plants with shrivelled, yellow or wilted leaves should be avoided.

If your transplant is in a peat pot, gently tear off the bottom or the side of the pot and release the roots unharmed. Although the roots will penetrate through the peat and the peat will eventually decompose, a dry period could keep roots pot-bound and hinder good development. Immediately after transplanting, water all plants thoroughly.

A well-stocked garden center like the one pictured is a convenient way to buy plants to add "instant" color to your garden with minimum effort.

Biggest causes of failure from this form of planting are generally dehydration (lack of adequate moisture at the time of planting or after planting) and planting too early with tender plants. Young plants are more susceptible to harm in the first seven days after transplanting than at any other time in their development. Tender plants, such as petunias, impatiens and begonias, should not be planted until all danger of frost is past.

Bulbs

Like seeds and transplants, there are tender varieties and hardy varieties of flowering bulbs, but both are easy to handle. A choice selection of the easiest-to-grow kinds are readily available at garden centers, hardware stores and supermarkets, but a greater selection is generally offered through specialist bulb catalogs. The spring-flowering kinds are offered in September for fall planting, while the summer-flowering kinds normally sell from April 1st for spring planting.

The biggest losses with bulbs are due to rotting, caused by poor drainage, and rodent damage (especially tulips and crocus).

Rooted Cuttings

Many kinds of perennials, such as chrysanthemums, and some plants classified as annuals, such as ageratum, can be purchased as rooted cuttings from garden centers and through the mail or can be started at home as a do-it-yourself project.

Cuttings can be made from sections of stem, which develop roots when in contact with moist soil, and from certain perennials like Carnations. With hybrids, propagation by cuttings is the only way to replicate the original plant, since seed from hybrids is often sterile or produces uncharacteristic plants.

When bought through the mail, cuttings will generally arrive bare-rooted and need to be kept constantly moist until time of transplanting.

Seeds

Seeds are generally the least expensive way to grow flowers. Some plants are easy to grow, others are more challenging. A choice selection of the most popular kinds of annuals and perennials are readily available from local retail outlets.

A wider selection is offered through mail-order catalogs, and this is a reliable way to buy seeds, since seeds are light and present no problems of handling through the U.S. mails.

Most hardy perennials and hardy annuals can be sown directly into the garden, but there are so many aids for starting seeds indoors that this is a preferred method. Seeds of tender plants and plants with tiny seeds should always be started indoors.

Bad seed is generally the least common cause of failure, since seed companies are empowered by law to test batches of seed *every year* and meet high germination and purity standards.

Starting Seeds Indoors

There are many beautiful kinds of flowers that should be started early indoors, either because they need a little longer growing period in which to reach flowering size or because the seeds are tiny and perishable if planted directly into the soil. Seed packets will generally give accurate instructions on the kinds of flowers that should be sown directly into the soil or started early indoors.

The old method of starting seeds was to use wooden seed flats filled with a planting mixture of equal parts sifted garden soil, sand and peat. The seeds were sown in straight furrows and thinned to gain a flat full of healthy transplants.

This old established method is still practiced by nurserymen in many parts of the country and by people with greenhouses and sufficient space to keep the large cumbersome seed flats. For the home gardener, however, the system has disadvantages. Garden soil unless it is sterilized by steaming can introduce a destructive fungus causing damping-off disease, which weakens plant stems at the soil line and causes them to perish. The average homeowner has no room to keep the seed flats until time of transplanting. Because of these problems, the seed industry has developed some new, labor saving, easier ways for home gardeners to start seed indoors.

Peat Pots

Peat pots like those shown are a good way to start many types of seeds. The pots are filled with a planting soil, then several seeds are sown on top and covered over. After the seeds have sprouted, the smaller seedlings can be thinned out to leave one sturdy, healthy plant to occupy the entire pot. The peat sides are porous, and the roots will penetrate right through. Although these peat walls will decompose in the soil given adequate moisture, it is a good policy at transplanting time to peel away the bottom of each pot to allow more freedom for the roots to grow deep into the soil. Peat pots are available in kit form with planting soil.

Above *Sifting soil into a seedling flat*

Below *Making seed furrows with a straight edge*

Peat Pellets

Peat pellets are another easy way to grow both large and small seeded varieties of flowers and vegetables. When water is added to the pellet, it immediately swells to seven times its original height. The soft moist peat then makes an ideal growing medium for many kinds of plants. At transplanting time the netting around the peat is easily removed to allow the roots complete freedom to grow. Petunias, marigolds and impatiens are examples of varieties which do especially well with this method. Peat pellets are available in kit form with plastic watering trays to hold the pellets. A new type of peat pellet without a net is also available.

Peat and Plastic Planters

Peat or plastic planters are good to start fine seeds, such as petunias and pansies. The usual method is to fill the planters with a pre-packaged soil mix, make several lines of furrows with a flat edge, and sow the seed thinly along the furrows. Keep moist with a fine spray and transfer the seedlings to individual positions when they have developed a true set of leaves.

Seed Tapes

Seed tapes save time in spacing certain flowers and vegetables, and planting them is easy either indoors in a seed tray or directly into the garden. All you have to do is dig a shallow furrow to the recommended depth, stretch the tape along the furrow, cover with fine soil, and water lightly each day until seeds sprout. The seeds are pre-spaced in the tape, which is soluble and disappears quickly once it is in the ground, leaving the seeds free to germinate. Try zinnias, marigolds and alyssum. Seed tapes are readily available both from mail-order seed catalogs and local stores.

Pre-Planters

Most stores during spring will sell pre-planted packs of popular flower seeds. These packs generally consist of a plastic container filled with planting soil and seeds pre-spaced for reliable germinattion. All that is needed to start growing is water. The packs are deep enough to allow plants to reach a good size before transplanting, and they fit easily on a windowsill. After transplanting the empty plastic pack can be saved and re-used.

Hardening Off

When you buy plants from a garden center or grow them at home, be sure that they are hardened off before they are set outdoors for the summer. Young plants grown indoors under warm, protective conditions should be set in a cold frame for several days to condition them, so that the shock of transplanting into the open garden doesn't weaken them. If you don't have a cold frame, set them outside during the daytime for several days before you leave them out at night too.

It is particularly important for petunias, marigolds, zinnias, impatiens, begonias, salvias and other warm weather plants to be hardened off this way, otherwise cold nights could cause them serious set-back.

Plants purchased from garden centers and other reliable sources generally have been properly hardened off. Those that haven't been can be recognized by shrivelled or drooping leaves and brown leaf edges.

Tender annuals like this bed of mixed impatiens should be hardened off before planting outdoors after all danger of frost. Begonias, petunias and coleus require similar care to prevent losses. Note that here impatiens are thriving in full sun — because the stone paving keeps the soil cool. A cool soil is the most important requirement for impatiens, which is why they do well in semi-shade.

Starting Hard-to-Start Seeds

Method 1

1. Pour seeds into teaspoon directly from packet.

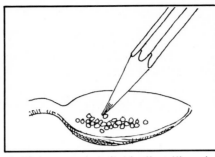

2. Pick up seeds individually with end of moist pencil.

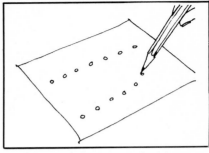

3. Place seeds in rows on moist paper towel.

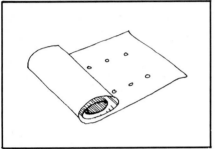

4. Roll towel loosely. Keep warm and moist. Most fine seeds need light to germinate.

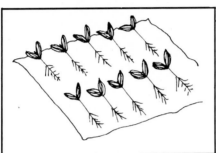

5. Examine towel after required germination period.

6. Use end of moist pencil and fore-finger to pick seedlings off towel. Transfer to individual peat pots.

Method 2

1. Sprinkle seeds on surface of peat pellet so surface is covered. Press seeds into surface lightly, but do not cover. Keep moist and warm.

2. When seeds have all sprouted, tear away the pellet netting.

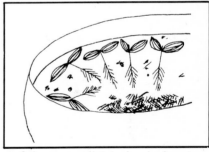

3. Submerge pellet in bowl of water. Soil and seedlings will separate. Seedlings will float.

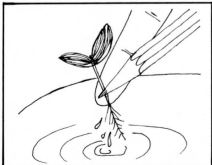

4. Using moist pencil point and fore-finger, gently lift seedlings in-dividually.

5. Transfer to individual peat pots filled with planting mix.

6. When plants reach transplanting size, peat pot can be planted directly into the garden to allow freedom for roots.

Helipterum   _Gaillardia Lollipops_   _Cleome Rose Queen_

Annuals for Sunny Places

In recent years, breeders have created many new annuals from flowers that were previously biennials or perennials, and among the major classes of annuals, some remarkable new varieties and sub-classes have come forward.

Among annuals that were converted from perennials and biennials we have _Foxy_ Foxglove, the first annual foxglove, Hibiscus _Southern Belle_ and Hollyhocks _Summer Carnival._

New sub-classes among the major annuals are _Peter Pan_ zinnias — a cross between the giant cactus-flowered types and dainty _Thumbelina._ Out of this marriage the Peter Pans produce large flowers on dwarf plants. They're early blooming, long lasting and make exceptional bedding plants.

Among snapdragons we not only have new forms in the familiar "dragon's mouth" type, but we have open-throated kinds and azalea-flowered forms, which look strikingly beautiful in flower arrangements.

In marigolds we have a new class called triploid hybrids. These are crosses between the dwarf French and tall American. They're earlier and longer lasting than their parents and create a more dense display of color. Because seed of these triploids is poor germinating, they should never be sown directly into the garden. They need coaxing indoors and then transplanting, but the extra trouble is well worth the effect.

Shade-loving annuals have been extensively improved, particularly the Big Three — begonia semperflorens, impatiens and coleus.

The F1 hybrid compact varieties of begonia semperflorens are so superior to standard varieties, I cannot imagine anyone wanting to grow other kinds. Tolerating shade, they also do well in full sun and give a continuous mound of bloom from spring until fall. Green foliaged and bronze foliaged types are available in a range of colors from dazzling white to bright pink to deep scarlet.

Both dwarf and semi-dwarf varieties of impatiens have been hybridized, and breeders will be concentrating their future efforts into producing even larger flowers. The _Elfins_ (dwarf) and _Imps_ (semi-dwarf) are two of the best varieties.

Among coleus, a new fringed class called the _Carefrees_ are making a big hit.

Breeders have also made astonishing improvements in dianthus, beginning with _Bravo,_ which a Japanese breeder found growing by the wayside and boosted from obscurity to overnight fame by entering it in the All-America Selections, where it won a silver medal. Today, using _Bravo_ as breeding material, we have a new range of hybrids, notably _Queen of Hearts,_ a scarlet red, and _Magic Charms,_ a mixture.

Ten years ago, a common criticism with petunias was the enormous number of new varieties released each year. With the breakthrough of _Fire Chief_ — the first truly red petunia — breeders had a new incentive to extend the color range. Soon every conceivable shape and color came forth among the four major classes — grandiflora singles, multiflora singles, grandiflora doubles and multiflora doubles. The fact remains, however, that breeders still feel there are big improvements to be made with petunias — particularly in terms of rain and pollution tolerance, better yellows, larger size and earliness.

As a result of recent travels to Europe and the Orient, I have seen some even greater flower improvements in the making, such as miniature roses which can be treated as annuals to bloom from seed in four months, and beautiful trumpet lilies which bloom from seed in six months. These are innovations beyond our wildest dreams, which convinces me that plant breeding has even greater discoveries in store.

Aster Early Bird

Alyssum Carpet of Snow

Ageratum Blue Blazer

Amaranthus Illumination

Note: A hardy annual has seeds that may be sown outdoors before danger of all spring frost has passed. A tender annual should not be sown outdoors before the last frost. Wait until the ground has warmed up thoroughly.

Ageratum

Ageratum Houstonianum. Tender annual, 3 to 12 in. high, blooming from early summer to autumn. Fluffy, floss-like flowers are mostly blue, although white (*Snowdrift*) and pink varieties (*Fairy Pink*) also exist.

Excellent for borders, edgings, window boxes and other containers. Combines well with marigolds and petunias.

Recommended varieties: *Blue Angel, Blue Blazer, Blue Chip* and *Blue Mink* — all F1 hybrids growing about 6 in. tall. *Midget Blue*, an All-America winner, grows to 3 in. Start seed indoors or purchase young plants after danger of frost has passed in spring.

Alyssum

Lobularia maritima. Hardy annual, 3 to 8 in. tall, blooming from early summer to autumn. Dainty, fragrant flowers are freely produced on mound-shaped plants. Tolerates heat and blooms quickly from seed. Colors include snow white, rose, pink and purple.

Possibly the most popular plant for edging a flower border. Excellent as a companion for taller plants in containers; also for rockeries and between stepping stones. Especially

beautiful when the white kinds are alternated with blue lobelia (*Lobelia Erinus*), another fine edging plant.

Carpet of Snow (4 in.) forms a dense low-spreading white mat. *Rosy O'Day* (3 in.) is a lovely deep rose and an All-America winner. *Royal Carpet* (3 in.), a violet-purple, is also an All-America winner. *Snowdrift* (3 in.) and *Oriental Night* (dwarf deep purple) are also very good. Quick and reliable when sown directly in the garden.

Amaranthus

Amaranthus tricolor (Summer Poinsettia). Tender annual, 3 to 4 ft. high, grown for its brilliant leaf colorings. Each stem is topped with a "crown" of cascading leaves in combinations of scarlet, green and yellow.

Excellent in beds as a highlight or as a background to lower growing annuals. Superb by itself or planted between shrubs, providing it receives plenty of sun. Blooms from July to fall frosts. Easily grown from seed sown outdoors after danger of frost, but transplanting speeds up leaf coloring.

Recommended varieties: *Molten Fire* (broad scarlet leaves) and *Illumination* with narrow leaves striped red and yellow.

Anchusa

Anchusa capensis (Summer or Cape Forget-me-not). Hardy annual, 6 to 18 in. tall, blooming from early summer to late autumn with clusters of small sky-blue flowers.

Blue Bird is a semi-dwarf and blends well as a companion plant with other annuals in the border. *Blue Angel* is dwarf and so compact that it may be treated as an edging plant like lobelia or ageratum.

Sow seed outdoors as soon as the soil is dry or start indoors to get healthy transplants.

Aster, China

Callistephus chinensis. Half-hardy annual, blooming from midsummer to autumn. It is among the ten most popular garden flowers in America, despite problems of wilt disease. Tall kinds make excellent cut flowers; in fact, entire plants may be uprooted for bouquets. They have the largest blue flowers of any annual. Other colors include white, rose-pink and crimson.

The following are popular wilt-resistant strains: *Giant Cregos*, with fluffy, informal flower stalks, growing 2 ft. tall with individual blossoms up to 5 in. across; *Powderpuffs*, with smaller, fully double flowers and quilled centers about 3 in. across; also, *Dwarf Queen* and *Color Carpet*, growing just 10 in. tall, an ideal size for low beds or edgings. Aster yellows and wilt are serious problems. Select wilt-resistant varieties and don't grow China asters in the same place two years in succession.

For earliest bloom, start seed indoors. It can also be direct-sown in the garden after danger of frost.

13

Ornamental Cabbage

Brachycombe (Swan River Daisy)

Balsam Camellia-flowered

Bachelor's Button Blue Diadem

Bachelor's Button

Centaurea cyanus (Cornflower). Hardy annual, 1-1/2 to 2-1/2 ft. tall, blooming early summer to autumn. Thrives in poor soil and withstands heat. Blue is the traditional color, but white, pink and red are also available, separately and in mixtures.

Decorative in a flower border, cornflowers are invaluable for cutting. *Snow Ball,* an All-America winner, is unusual because its pure white flowers grow on dense plants, just 1 ft. tall, with such profusion they create a mound effect.

Quick and easy to raise from seed sown directly in the garden. Sow some seed in fall for early flowering the following year.

Balsam

Impatiens Balsamina. Tender annual, 18 in. tall, growing fleshy stems crowded with double flowers resembling miniature camellias in white, pink, red and purple, including some striped bicolors. Blooms July through September and tolerates light shade. Prefers a rich, moist soil.

Good for beds and borders. Recommended varieties: *Double Camellia-flowered Mixed* and *Tom Thumb,* a good dwarf strain.

Seed can be sown outdoors after danger of frost, although starting indoors and transplanting is better.

Basil, Ornamental

Ocimum Basilicum. Tender annual, 15 in. high, grown for its richly colored deep purple foliage.

In 1949, a plant finding expedition to Turkey — sponsored by the United States Department of Agriculture — returned with specimens of a new unusual variety of basil. The University of Connecticut observed a unique purple foliage that was characteristic of some of the plants, and after several generations of selection, they developed a true breeding line called *Dark Opal.*

Although the variety showed it was edible as an herb — just like normal basil — the scientists decided it had value as an ornamental plant in the flower garden and in 1960 entered it in All-America Selections. It promptly carried off a bronze medal and has since proved invaluable for garden display, especially as a background to low-growing plants, such as dwarf marigolds.

Dark Opal grows easily from seed planted directly into the garden after danger of frost, or from transplants.

Bells of Ireland

Molucella laevis. Half-hardy annual, 10 to 36 in. tall, blooming from mid to late summer. Stems are closely set with decorative green, bell-shaped bracts and a dainty white flower at the center. Does best in full sun and tolerates heat. Decorative in a border, Bells of Ireland are principally grown for cutting to make attractive arrangements.

Seed is hard-skinned and sensitive to cold. Normally does well direct-sown into the garden, given plenty of moisture after the soil has become thoroughly warm.

Brachycome

Brachycome iberidifolia (Swan River Daisy). Tender annual, growing 10 in. high, flowering July and August. Creates a dense bush of daisy-like blooms in white, rose, blue and purple, resembling Michaelmas Daisies.

Enjoys a sunny location and grows easily from seed sown outdoors in May after danger of frost. Superb plants for borders and rock gardens, spaced 15 in. apart. One of the finest flowering annuals ever to come out of Australia.

Browallia

Browallia americana. Tender annual, 12 in. high, flowering outdoors July until fall frost. Good for borders, but especially desirable as a container planting or hanging basket subject. Flowers are sapphire blue and white in such profusion they will completely hide the container when well grown.

Calendula Pacific Beauty

Calliopsis   California-poppy Mission Bells   Calceolaria rugosa

Tolerates shade and is widely used as an indoor plant. Prefers a light, moist soil. Recommended varieties: *Sapphire* and *Silver Bells*.

Start indoors in April for transplanting outside in May after danger of frost or sow seed directly into the garden.

Cabbage, Ornamental

Ornamental Cabbage (Flowering Kale). Hardy annual growing 1 ft. high, spreading 1-1/2 ft. Except in areas of coastal California, the Pacific Northwest and coastal Maine, the best way to grow ornamental cabbage is as a fall display flower, setting out transplants into flowering positions in August so that they mature during cool fall weather.

The exquisite pink and white frilly coloring of the central leaves will color-up only during cool weather. Use them in massed beds, as an edging of all one color or alternating colors (white and pink), and in window boxes.

Start seed indoors in early summer or outside in a shaded position to get transplants several inches high for setting into flowering positions spaced 1 ft. apart.

Calceolaria

Calceolaria rugosa (Purse Flower). Tender annual, 12 to 18 in. high, grown mostly as an indoor flowering houseplant.

However, a new dwarf hybrid variety called *Sunshine* has proved successful for outdoor flower beds and containers, especially window boxes.

Blooms of *Sunshine* are rounded, shaped like a purse, and highly unusual. Color is bright yellow, with hundreds of flowers open at one time on bushy, compact plants, blooming over a long period from July to September.

Best to start seed indoors in January and February at 60 degrees for transplanting after danger of frost. Especially good for cooler locations.

Calendula

Calendula officinalis. Half-hardy annual, 12 to 24 in. tall, mostly in yellow, apricot and orange, blooming from spring to autumn. Performs best during cool months. Leaves have a pleasant, spicy odor. Attractive in a border, calendula also makes a good cut flower.

Pacific Beauty strain (18 in.) is notable. Seems to resist heat better than most. Lower-growing varieties are also available.

Easy to grow from seed directly sown in the garden. Will reseed itself year after year in most areas.

California-poppy

Eschscholzia californica. Hardy annual, 10 to 12 in. tall,

blooming from spring to early summer, but thriving best in the cooler weather of spring. Grow it in a sunny location and give it sandy soil. Plants have a spreading habit, and the poppy-like petals shine with a satin texture. Golden-yellow flowers are the most common; good mixtures contain cream, yellow, orange, pink, rose and scarlet.

A good companion for other spring bloomers; also lends itself to naturalizing.

Monarch and *Mission Bells* are superior mixtures.

Sow directly into the garden where the plants are to bloom. Recommended for autumn sowing in all but the coldest areas.

Calliopsis

Coreopsis tinctoria. Hardy annual, 9 to 36 in. tall, blooming in summer. Plants grow best in a sunny location, tolerate heat, resist drought and thrive even in poor soils. The bright, daisy-like flowers are yellow, orange or red and bi-colored. Available usually in mixtures, but color selections have been made.

Dwarf varieties, which are fine for borders, form neat mounds 10 or 12 in. high; tall kinds are excellent for cutting.

Easy to grow and quick to flower when sown directly in the garden.

Celosia Fireglow

Dianthus Merry-Go-Round

Dahlia Sunburst

Cosmos Radiance

Celosia

Celosia argentea cristata (Cockscomb); *Celosia argentea plumosa* (Plumed). Tender annual, 6 in. to 3 ft. tall, blooming midsummer to autumn. Two types are popular — the cockscomb (crested) and the plumed. Gold, yellow, pink, rose and red are the basic colors. Both kinds need a warm, sunny location for vivid display. Dwarf celosias are excellent for edging, while tall ones are effective in borders and make dramatic cut flowers, both fresh and dried.

Breeders have made significant improvements in this old-time garden favorite. Two notable cockscombs, All-America winners, are *Fireglow,* with cardinal-red globe-shaped blooms, and *Toreador,* with gigantic red combs up to 9 in. across. Among plumed kinds to win All-America awards are *Golden Triumph* (2-1/2 ft. tall) with its striking golden-yellow plumes, and *Red Fox* (1-1/2 ft. tall), which is carmine red.

Celosia grows quickly, thrives in heat, and resists drought. Seed can be direct-sown in the garden or started indoors for earlier flowering, but care should be taken that growth is not checked; otherwise, poor bloom may result.

Clarkia

Clarkia elegans. Hardy annual, 2 ft. tall, flowering July to October. Delicate, double flowers grow closely packed along slender stems. Colors include white, pink, red and mauve.

For earliest blooms sow seed indoors in March and transplant 9 in. apart in May. Likes a cool, semi-shaded location.

Cleome

Cleome spinosa (Spider Plant). Half-hardy annual, 4 ft. tall, blooming from midsummer until autumn on slender stems topped with a white or pink crown of flowers.

Attractive in large groups in the border and as a background for lower-growing annuals. Useful as a temporary screen, and sometimes planted between tall shrubs. *Helen Campbell,* a pure white, and *Rose Queen,* a deep pink, are good varieties.

Can be direct-sown, but starting indoors will result in earlier blooms.

Cosmos

Cosmos bipinnatus. Half-hardy annual, 3 ft. tall, with feathery foliage and masses of summer flowers in white, rose, pink, crimson, yellow and orange-red depending on species. Thrives in average soil and tolerates heat. Give it full sun. Usually needs staking, but exceptional as a border plant and wonderful for cutting.

Three All-America winners: *Radiance,* a deep rose with crimson zone around a golden-yellow center; *Sunset,* a deep orange; and *Diablo,* a glowing reddish-orange.

Anyone can grow cosmos. Sow seed directly in the garden after frost or start it indoors for earlier flowering.

Dahlia

Dahlia pinnata. Tender annual, 2 to 5 ft. tall, blooming midsummer until autumn in full sun. Requires good soil. Both green- and bronze-leaved varieties are available in a spectacular range and combination of colors (except blue).

Kinds grown widely from seed include the miniature pompom dahlias (3 ft.), which have ballshaped flowers, the *Unwin* type (2 ft.) with double and semi-double blooms having smooth or fluted petals, and the large-flowered cactus sort (5 ft.) All are beautiful in borders as a background planting and mixed with other annuals in large containers.

Seed of most dahlias is best started early indoors to get good-sized plants for earlier bloom. Dwarf kinds — such as the All-America winner, *Redskin,* with bronze foliage — can be direct-sown after the soil has warmed up. Flowering is usually best in autumn.

Dianthus

Dianthus chinensis (Pinks). Hardy annual, 8 to 18 in. tall, blooming June until autumn. Forms perfect mounds of refined foliage and colorful flowers, some smooth petaled, others serrated, in white, pink and red, plus combinations of these colors. Grow in full sun. Tolerates poor or sandy soil.

Dimorphotheca (African Daisies)

Felicia (Kingfisher Daisy)

Dusty Miller (Cineraria Diamond)

Euphorbia

Useful as edgings, also in borders and rock gardens. In recent years breeders have developed outstanding varieties with showier flowers and longer bloom period. Notable All-America winners: *Bravo* (red), *Queen of Hearts* (a red hybrid), *China Doll* (double-flowered mixture with fringed petals), *Magic Charms* (first hybrid mixture) and *Snowfire* (bi-colored white and red).

Advisable to start indoors, but direct-sowing can be satisfactory, too. Best flowering is in the cool weather of early summer and autumn. Flowers as a perennial in subsequent years, especially if plants are sheared back after fall flowering.

Annual varieties of dianthus sown from seed will germinate easily at a wide range of temperatures, although 70 degrees is the optimum. After germination, 40 degrees to 65 degrees is the ideal growing range. Under good light conditions, first flowers will appear in 12 to 14 weeks.

Dianthus is sensitive to ammonia damage, causing leaf tip burn, so organic or ammonia derived fertilizers should be used sparingly.

Dimorphotheca
Dimorphotheca aurantiaca (African Daisy). Tender annual, 12 in. tall, flowering all summer with single daisy-like flowers in white, yellow, apricot, orange and bicolors.

Useful in low beds and borders. Needs a sunny location,

succeeds in a wide range of soils including poor soil, tolerates drought, but blooms more profusely during cool, sunny weather.

Start seed indoors in March or April, or sow outdoors in May.

Dusty Miller
Centauria and Cineraria species. There are several species of plants commonly called *Dusty Miller* because of the "woolly" silvery texture of the leaves, the main species being *cineraria* and *centauria*.

Most widely used of all, however, is a variety of *cineraria* called *Silverdust,* best treated as a tender annual, growing 8 in. tall, with bright silver foliage, beautifully fringed and cut. Effective for edging flower beds and borders, particularly as a contrast to red petunias and geraniums.

Plants are readily available from garden centers in spring or seed can be sown in February to get good size transplants for setting into the garden after danger of frost.

Euphorbia
Euphorbia marginata (Snow-on-the-Mountain). Hardy annual, 2 ft. tall, grown for its light green leaves, which are striped with white. An eye-catching foliage plant for borders and strategic places among shrubs. Likes full sun and does well even in poor soil.

Easily grown from seed sown directly into the garden in April or May, creating its best effect in July and August. The fleshy stems are good for cutting as indoor flower arrangements, but care should be taken to keep the milky sap away from cuts and eyes, since it can cause skin irritations.

Felicia
Felicia Bergeriana (Kingfisher Daisy). Tender annual, 6 in. high, producing brilliant blue daisy flowers with golden-yellow centers. Needs full sun and prefers a dry soil.

Start seeds indoors in March for transplanting outdoors after danger of frost.

Forget-Me-Not
Myosotis oblongata and alpestris. *Alpestris* varieties of forget-me-not are hardy biennials, requiring two seasons to flower. *Oblongata Blue Bird,* however, is a variety that can be grown as an annual. Also widely used for forcing as winter and spring pot plants or for cutting.

Alpestris varieties can be sown outdoors from June to August and transplanted to flowering positions in fall. They make especially fine companion plants bedded among spring-flowering tulips, flowering April to June.

Recommended *alpestris* variety: *Blue Ball,* growing compact, bushy plants no more than 6 in. high.

Carefree Geraniums   *Gazanias*   *Four O'Clocks Jingles*

Four O'clock

Mirabilis Jalapa. Best treated as a tender annual, 2 ft. tall, blooming midsummer to autumn in all colors except blue. Some flowers are even striped. Grow in a sunny location. This old-time favorite takes heat, drought and poor soil. Bush plants are covered with flowers which open in the afternoon on sunny days and stay open all day on cloudy days. Useful as a border plant, or as a temporary hedge.

Easy to grow, but best from seed started indoors. Seedlings frequently appear in the garden in succeeding years if winters are mild. Occasionally the tuberous roots will live over the winter if frost has not deeply penetrated the soil.

Gaillardia

Gaillardia pulchella. Hardy annual, 14 to 24 in., blooming early summer to autumn. Survives heat, drought and poor soils. Single and double forms come in colors of yellow, orange, maroon, scarlet and combinations of these.

Good in the flower border for display and cutting. *Gaiety* (2 ft.), with double flowers in mixed colors, and *Lollipop* series (14 in.), in mixed or separate colors, are recommended.

Sow directly in the garden or start plants early indoors.

Gazania

Gazania splendens. Tender annual, 8 in. tall, flowering July to September. The single, daisy-like flowers shimmer in the sunlight in a beautiful range of colors including white, yellow, orange, red, pink and bronze. The petals are generally bicolored with contrasting "zones" close to the center.

Useful in rock gardens and as an edging. Tolerates drought and poor soil, but flowers have the annoying habit of closing up on cloudy days or when shaded. The seeds are unusual, embedded in fluff, and need to be separated for sowing. Best grown indoors in total darkness for 7 days, then transplanted after danger of frost.

Recommended variety: *Sunshine Hybrids,* a really fine color mixture.

Geranium

Pelargonium hortorum. Until 10 years ago, geraniums grown from seed could not be grown true to color. In other words, seed saved from a pink geranium would just as likely produce a white or red flower.

This characteristic was particularly disappointing because home gardeners do not like to grow geraniums as mixtures. So the only way to grow single colors was from costly cuttings.

Then plant breeders at Penn State University discovered how to produce hybrids that not only grew true to color from seed, but gave a better display and flowered earlier than standard varieties.

Next came the "Carefree" family of hybrid geraniums, with three of the colors — Scarlet, Bright Pink and Salmon — gaining awards of recognition in All-America Selections.

The next breakthrough was a magnificent scarlet red called *Sprinter* — the most popular of all geranium colors, and it promptly carried off awards in both Fleuro-select (the European flower trials) and All Britain Trials.

Sprinter has proved to be as much as 2 weeks earlier than any other geranium grown from seed. As an added bonus, it is also more dwarf than other varieties, averaging 1-1/2 ft. high. Just 12 weeks are needed from sowing the seed to first blooms. Sown indoors in February, transplants beginning to show color are ready by May 15th to give a continuous display of color well into fall.

Sprinter has a natural branching habit from the base of the plant, allowing each plant to produce many more flowers than other geraniums.

Optimum germination for the seed is 70-75 degrees. The seed is easy to grow because it is *scarified* to aid germination. (Scarifying is a technique whereby the coats of seeds with hard skins are shaved to aid moisture penetration.)

18

Gomphrena (Globe Amaranth)   Godetia Gem   Ornamental Gourds

For gardeners who prefer to buy geranium plants ready grown, they are available by variety name from nurseries and garden centers.

Godetia

Godetia amoena. Hardy annual, 8 to 24 in. high, flowering in cool weather from July to fall frost. Many travelers to Northern Europe who see these plants flowering profusely with a satin texture on mound-shaped plants feel tempted to try them at home in the United States. Apart from parts of Canada and the Pacific Northwest, however, they generally give a poor display. Given cool, sunny conditions they will grow in poor soil and seem to enjoy being crowded.

Sown outdoors in May, plants will bloom in 70 days.

Gomphrena

Gomphrena globosa (Globe Amaranth). Tender annual, 6 to 18 in. high, blooming from July until fall. The globular flowers resemble clover heads in white, purple and red shades.

Good for rock gardens and sunny flower beds, especially the dwarf purple variety called *Dwarf Buddy.* Seeds are best started indoors in March in total darkness at 80 degree soil temperature until germination.

Flower heads have a papery texture and dry easily to make effective everlasting arrangements.

Gourds, Ornamental

Cucurbita pepo ovifera (small gourds); *Lagenaria vulgaris* (large gourds). Tender annuals, vining 12 ft. and producing decorative fruits in late summer or early autumn. Thrive in full sun and rich soil. Can be trained to grow up a trellis.

Small kinds are the most widely grown, since the ripened fruits can be quickly dried and varnished to make beautiful ornaments in color combinations of yellow, orange, green and white, and shapes ranging from apple, orange and pear to eggs. Some even resemble miniature bottles.

Sow directly in the garden after all danger of frost. Grow as you would pumpkin or squash. *Lagenaria vulgaris* are the kind to grow for bird boxes and dippers.

Gypsophila, Annual

Gypsophila elegans (Baby's Breath). Hardy annual, 6 in. to 3 ft. with white or pink flowers. Short bloom season, but flowers are dainty and profuse, giving a lacy effect.

Useful in the cutting garden, for it provides an excellent contrast in arrangements with zinnias, marigolds and other vividly colored flowers. Recommended variety: *Covent Garden White* (1-1/2 ft.), with large flowers for a gypsophila.

Easily grown in any soil and quick to bloom. Sow directly in

the garden or start indoors for early flowering.

Heliotrope

Heliotrope arborescens. Hardy annual, 15 in. high, flowering June to fall frosts. Flowers are sweetly scented, imparting a fragrance similar to vanilla. The flower heads form large mound-shaped panicles in white, blue and violet-purple against deep green foliage.

Prefers a sunny location in rich, well-drained soil. Start indoors in March to gain healthy transplants or sow directly into the garden after danger of frost, spacing plants 18 in. apart.

Recommended variety: *Marine,* colored a rich violet and especially attractive when dried for everlasting arrangements.

Helipterum

Helipterum roseum (Acroclinium). Hardy annual, 15 in. high, flowering July and August. Flowers resemble daisies in white and pink with gorgeous yellow centers. Strawy texture of petals assures long life first as a freshly cut flower, and then as a dried flower in everlasting flower arrangements.

Sow seeds directly into the garden in May, thinning to 6 in. apart. Likes a sunny position and light soil.

Kochia

Impatiens and Lobelia

Hibiscus Southern Belle

Hollyhock Summer Carnival

Hibiscus Southern Belle

Hibiscus Moscheutos selection.
Can be treated as an annual, blooming late summer to autumn on bushy, 5-ft. tall plants. The flowers, up to 10 in. across, are white, rose and crimson with contrasting centers. Seed packets contain mixed colors.

Southern Belle, an All-America winner, has a striking, tropical appearance. Use it as a focal point in the garden or at the edge of a pond or stream.

To get flowers the first year, seed must be sown indoors early (January or February) for transplanting when plants are a foot high after danger of frost. Requires 70 degree temperature to germinate. After frost in the autumn, plants die back. Except in very cold areas, if given protection, they will make new growth the following spring and perform as a hardy perennial thereafter.

Hollyhock

Althaea rosea. Hardy annual, 2 to 6 ft. tall, blooming from midsummer to autumn on slender stems surrounded by single or double flowers in white, yellow, pink and red. Grow in a sunny location sheltered from wind. Tall kinds often need staking.

Useful as a tall background plant. Hollyhock is a biennial, or short-lived perennial, but plant breeders have developed a few annual types of this old favorite. Notable All-America winners include *Majorette,* the first dwarf hollyhock mixture (2 ft. tall), and *Summer Carnival* (5 ft.), a superb early-flowering mixture. Both are double-flowered.

Although seed can be sown directly in the garden, it is best to start them early indoors.

Kochia

Kochia Childsii. Tender annual, 3 ft. tall, grown for its feathery "evergreen" foliage which lasts from midsummer until fall, changing from light green to red. Likes sun, takes heat, drought and poor soil.

Widely used as a temporary hedge and as a background planting in combination with colorful annuals such as marigolds, zinnias and petunias.

Sow seed directly into the garden or start early indoors for transplanting.

Larkspur

Delphinium Ajacis. Hardy annual, 3 to 4 ft. tall, blooming late spring to midsummer. The bushy plants produce masses of flower spikes in white, blue and pink. Best in sun, but will take a little shade. Staking is often necessary.

Good for backgrounds and borders, also an excellent cut flower. Deep watering in dry weather helps prolong bloom period.

Grows quickly from direct sowings if planted as early in the spring as possible. Cool weather favors good germination, rapid growth and profuse flowering.

Linum

Linum grandiflorum rubrum (Scarlet Flax). Although there are many kinds of perennial and annual linum, by far the most beautiful is the scarlet form, *grandiflorum rubrum,* an easy-to-grow hardy annual, creating masses of shiny flowers 1-1/2 in. across on 1-1/2 ft. stems, flowering from June to fall.

Tolerates a wide range of soil conditions in an open, sunny location. Seeds can be sown out-

Marigold Jubilee

Marigold Dainty Marietta

Marigold Bolero

Matricaria Snowball

doors in blooming positions during April and May.

Lobelia

Lobelia Erinus. Tender annual, 4 to 6 in. tall, flowering July to September, each plant covered with myriads of dainty flowers.

Dwarf compact types, such as *Mrs. Clibran* (dark blue) and *Rosamund* (a red All-America winner), are excellent for edging borders. Trailing types, such as *Blue Cascade* and *Red Cascade,* are excellent for hanging baskets or combining with other summer-flowering annuals in container plantings. Does well in semi-shade.

Since seed is very tiny and growth is slow, plants are best bought from garden centers in spring. Otherwise start seed indoors before March 15th to get decent-size plants for transplanting.

Marigold

Tagetes erecta (American); *Tagetes patula* (French). Half-hardy annual, 6 in. to 3-1/2 ft., blooming late spring to autumn. Flowers single or double, in vàrious sizes and shapes. Yellow, orange and rusty-red are the

basic hues, which are vivid, and there are bicolors. Tolerant of drought and poor soil. Insect and garden pests seem to avoid marigolds because of their spicy odor. Popular among vegetable gardeners, who interplant them among cabbage and beans for protection from rabbits. The roots also repel nematodes.

Probably no garden flower is less trouble to grow, has a longer period of bloom or has more decorative value, both inside and outside the home, than the marigold. There are two kinds — the dwarf French and tall African (American).

French marigolds are versatile in borders and used as any low-growing annual would be. Good for containers, too. There are numerous varieties and forms. Two excellent kinds are *Gypsy* and *Petite. Dainty Marietta* is single-flowered, a lovely red and yellow bicolor with a daisy-like appearance. Choice larger-flowered kinds include *Bolero* (All-America winner), *Carmen, Fiesta, Red Brocade* and *Sparky.*

The largest-flowered African (or American) marigolds, which

bloom later in the summer, are the *Jubilee, Crackerjack* and *Climax* series. The first grows 2 ft. tall, the others to 3 ft. An outstanding All-America winner is *Showboat,* a dwarf triploid. Dwarf Triploids are crosses between the French and African, producing large, long-lasting dense blooms on low-growing plants.

Seed of all except triploid hybrids does well direct-sown into the garden, although starting indoors is recommended for earlier blooms.

Matricaria

Matricaria Chamomilla (Feverfew). Hardy annual, 8 to 23 in. high, flowering July, August and September. The bushy plants are covered with button-type flowers, resembling miniature chrysanthemums, in yellow and white.

Good for border display and as a cut flower. Likes sun and any well-drained soil. Sow indoors February 1st for June flowering or outdoors after danger of frost for August blooms.

Recommended variety: *Golden Ball.*

21

Mesembryanthemum   Nicotiana Daylight   Nasturtium Dwarf Jewel

Mesembryanthemum

Mesembryanthemum crinifolium
(Livingstone Daisy).   Tender
annual growing 3 in. high,
flowering midsummer in cool,
sunny regions. Creates a low,
spreading mass of succulent
plants with brilliant daisy-like
flowers in red, pink, carmine,
magenta and orange.

These brilliantly colored
plants thrive in a sunny, exposed
location in dry soils, especially in
cool coastal areas. Start seeds
indoors in early spring, transplanting the seedlings to their
permanent locations after danger
of frost. Very popular in coastal
California and the Pacific Northwest where cool, sunny conditions
present a perfect environment.

Mignonette

Reseda odorata.   Tender
annual, 12 to 18 in. high. Not a
display flower, but its delightful
fragrance is good enough reason
to grow it, and although it prefers
full sun, it will tolerate light
shade.

Has a romantic history few
other flowers can match. The
famous French emperor,
Napoleon, saw the plant growing
along the banks of the Nile
during his attempted conquest of
Egypt. He was fascinated by its
delightful fragrance and sent
some seeds to his Empress,
Josephine. She was an avid
gardener and grew the new plant

under her bedroom window in a
window box. She loved its
unusual fragrance so much she
made it fashionable throughout
France to grow it, and soon its
popularity spread to other
countries.

Sow seeds directly into the
garden after danger of frost, and
plant in patches among non-
fragrant annuals in a window box
or near a doorway. Bring the fragrance indoors by cutting
bunches and arranging them in a
bowl. They last nearly a week and
mix well with more colorful
annuals, such as marigolds and
zinnias.

Mimulus

Mimulus luteus (Monkey
Flower).   Tender annual,
growing 1-1/2 ft. high, producing
bushy, mound-shaped plants
covered in trumpet-shaped yellow
flowers handsomely blotched
with red markings.

Demands a cool soil and a
sunny location. Seeds should be
started indoors in March or April
and planted out after danger of
frost. Does especially well close to
ponds and streams or in island
beds surrounded by flagstone
where cool soil conditions prevail.

Nasturtium

Tropaeolum majus. Half-hardy
annual, 12 in. to 3 ft. blooming
early summer to fall. Needs full
sun and does well in heat,

drought and poor soil. Colors
predominate in yellow, orange
and red.

Dwarf varieties are good for
borders, containers and rock
gardens. Trailing kinds will
climb up a trellis, cascade over
window boxes and cover banks.
The flowers make lovely indoor
arrangements, and the whole
plant is good to eat. The stems,
flowers and leaves have a spicy
taste similar to garden cress and
are delicious in salads. Seeds may
be pickled in vinegar.

Double dwarf *Jewel* and
semi-tall *Gleam,* both in separate
or mixed colors, are recommended kinds. *Alaska* has
beautiful variegated leaves.

Sow seed directly in the
garden or start early indoors. Do
not plant in an overly rich soil, as
it encourages foliage at the
expense of bloom.

Nicotiana

Nicotiana alata.   Half-hardy
annual, 1 to 3 ft. tall, blooming
midsummer to fall. Thrives in
sun, but will tolerate part shade.
Resists heat and drought, and
performs satisfactorily in poor
soil. The fragrant, star-shaped
flowers grow at the ends of long
stems on bushy plants that bloom
early and freely all season. Colors
include crimson, pink and white.
Leaves are large, almost bold.
Nicotiana, known to many gardeners as flowering tobacco, is

Pansy Delft Blue   Grandiflora Double Petunia   Petunia White Cascade

Petunia Pink Joy

useful in the middle or back of the border and as a cut flower.

Primarily an evening bloomer, with flowers closing in sun. Exception to this is the *Daylight* strain. Lower-growing varieties of nicotiana, including *Crimson Bedder* and *White Bedder,* both 12 to 18 inches, are popular. One variety, *Lime Sherbet,* has yellow-green flowers.

Seed can be sown directly in the ground after danger of frost or started indoors. Volunteers frequently appear in succeeding years.

Pansies

Viola tricolor hortensis. Strictly speaking pansies are biennials, but in recent years flower breeders have produced new hybrids which are so vigorous and early to bloom they can be treated as hardy annuals. Growing 6 to 8 in. tall, pansies prefer the cool weather from early spring to early summer, but some of the new hybrids resist the heat and will flower continuously all summer right into fall. In color range, pansies are the most diverse of any annual flower, including red, white, blue and yellow, some handsomely blotched with black "faces".

They are invaluable for beds, edgings, borders, rock gardens and container plantings. They are attractive when com-
bined with spring-flowering bulbs, such as daffodils and tulips, and make dainty flower arrangements or "posies". *Majestic Giants Mixed Colors* are an All-America Award winner and a magnificent hybrid mixture. Also look for a new race of hybrids called the "Imperials", especially *Imperial Blue,* an All-America winner, which is the most heat resistant and free-flowering of all pansies.

For spring blooms in the north, sow hybrid pansy seed indoors in January or February. Sow older varieties in midsummer in a cold frame or seed bed with the object of getting ready-to-bloom plants when winter sets in and holds them back. Then the first warm days of spring will bring them into magnificent early bloom.

Petunia

Petunia hybrida. Half-hardy annuals, 1 to 2 ft., and flowering midsummer to fall in an extensive color range including some beautiful bicolors. Useful for borders, edgings, window boxes, pots and other container plantings. The four most popular classes of petunia are the grandiflora single-flowered (giant, flat flowers), the multiflora singles (smaller-flowered, but more of them and providing a greater density of color), the grandiflora doubles and the multiflora
doubles.

Look in any seed catalog and you will find that petunias have the most extensive listing of varieties to choose from. Hybridizers still consider there are many improvements to be made, and choice of varieties is very much a personal matter. However, some outstanding selections are *Burgundy* (velvety deep purple, heavily veined grandiflora), *White Cascade* (gigantic ruffled grandiflora), and *Appleblossom* (lovely frilled appleblossom pink grandiflora, and an All-America winner). Among multifloras, *Comanche* (red) and *Coral Satin* are two All-America winners. In doubles, *Circus* is a beautiful bicolored red-and-white grandiflora (also an All-America winner).

For best results petunias should have full or nearly full sun. They thrive with frequent watering, but don't drench the delicate flowers.

Seed is tiny and should be started indoors, or young plants can be purchased after danger of frost has passed. The double-flowering sorts are challenging to germinate. Sprinkle their seeds sparingly on a wad of tissue paper and make it into a roll, keeping it moist and warm. After the tiny seedlings have sprouted, transfer them with care to individual peat pots for transplanting later.

Ricinus

Portulaca Sunshine Hybrids

Shirley Poppies

Phlox Dwarf Beauty

Phlox

Phlox Drummondii. Half-hardy annual, 7 to 15 in. high, blooming from early summer to autumn in an extensive color range, excluding true yellow and orange. Thrives in full sun and takes the heat.

Use tall kinds in borders, low-growing ones as edgings in borders and in container plantings. All-America winners: *Glamour* (15 in.), bearing large salmon flowers ideal for cutting; *Twinkle* (7 in.), a dwarf mixture having an almost endless variety of colors. Some of the flowers are delightfully fringed, others star-shaped, and many in two-color combinations.

Can be sown directly in the garden or started indoors.

Poppy, Shirley

Papaver Rhoeas. Hardy annual, 1-1/2 ft. tall, blooming early summer to fall. The delicate, brightly colored flowers are produced in many shades of pink, salmon, apricot and red, some edged in another color to create a two-tone effect. The large golden-yellow anthers create a lovely contrast. Useful in borders and for naturalizing on a sunny bank.

Poppies are best direct-sown into the garden, producing their best floral display during cool weather.

Portulaca

Portulaca grandiflora. Tender annual, 6 inches, blooming from early summer to autumn, but best in the hottest months. If you have a hot, dry part of the garden that needs brightening, try portulaca. Sometimes called moss-rose because the flowers resemble miniature rose blossoms, it is a low-growing, fleshy-stemmed, tender annual.

Flowers single or double, from white and yellow to pink and red, available in mixtures or separately. Typically the blossoms close at night and on cloudy days. Portulaca requires full sun and tolerates poor soil.

Quick and easy from seed sown in the garden well after danger of frost has passed. Scatter the tiny seed very thinly.

Ricinus

Ricinus communis (Castor Oil Plant). Tender annual, 8 to 15 ft. tall, grown for its lush tropical-looking foliage that looks most spectacular in July and August. Needs plenty of room, but has its place in home gardens as a lawn centerpiece or up against the house as a domineering highlight.

The large, freckled bean-size seeds are highly ornamental and good for making seed necklaces, but they are poisonous, forming the basis for mole bait, and should be kept out of reach of children.

Start seeds indoors in peat pots by May 1st, transplanting outdoors June 1st.

Salpiglossis

Salpiglossis sinuata. Half-hardy annual, 2-1/2 feet tall, blooming from midsummer to autumn. The brilliantly colored petunia-like flowers have a velvety texture and are heavily veined in contrasting colors. Principal flower colors are yellow, orange, red, pink and purple, commonly sold in mixtures. Excellent display flower in the garden and useful for cutting, although it does not do well everywhere, preferring cool summers of the Pacific Northwest and areas with similar conditions. Sow seeds indoors March 1st for earliest summer blooms at 80 degree soil temperature for 20 days in total darkness, pressing

Salvia Early Bonfire

Snapdragon Yellow Supreme

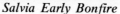

the tiny seeds into the soil surface, but not covering. Sowing outdoors can be made in late May.

Salvia

Salvia splendens (Scarlet Sage). Tender annual, 7 to 24 in. tall, blooming from early summer to autumn. Mostly grown for its blazing red flower spikes, but pink and blue varieties are available. Takes heat, drought and poor soil. Invaluable for edgings, borders, beds and container plantings. Many varieties in different sizes and hues are available.

Start seed indoors or purchase young plants in spring.

Schizanthus

Schizanthus pinnatus (Butterfly Flower). Half-hardy annual, growing to 18 in. high, flowering June, July and August. Extensive color range includes white, pink, yellow, rose, red, purple and many bicolors. Dozens of flowers bloom all at one time.

In northern areas of Europe, Canada and the cooler climates of the United States, they are an extremely worthwhile bedding plant, lasting a long time. Also the dwarf varieties make colorful

pot plants grown in a greenhouse during winter.

Recommended variety: *Hit Parade,* a dwarf strain growing large flowers.

Start seed indoors in February for planting outside after danger of frost. Seed sown outside May 1st will bloom in July. Very easy to grow from seed, but must have cool conditions and a sunny location.

Snapdragon

Antirrhinum majus. Treated as a hardy annual, 6 in. to 3 ft. tall, blooming best in the cool spring and autumn months. The flowers, on spikes, are all colors except blue. A good border plant and excellent for flower arrangements.

Hybridization has produced spectacular kinds. *Rocket* and *Topper* strains, in mixed or separate colors, are the tallest; plants are vigorous and produce 3-ft. spikes with up to 100 flowers and buds on a stem. *Butterfly* and *Bellflower* strains are novel. Their flowers have flared, wide-open throats instead of the tight-lipped kinds more common among snapdragon. Especially good for arrangements. *Floral Carpet,* in mixed or separate colors, grows 6 to 7 inches and is fine for a low-growing carpet.

Each plant has up to 25 tiny 3-in. spikes.

For a magnificent display start seed indoors early. Young plants may also be purchased in spring from a garden center or nursery. Snapdragons usually stop flowering in midsummer, but if old spikes are sheared back, they will make new growth in late summer and provide another colorful display well into autumn.

Stock

Matthiola incana. Hardy annual, 1 to 2 ft. tall, blooming from spring to early summer. The fragrant flowers are borne on heavy spikes. Colors are wine red, royal purple, white and pink, usually available in a mixture. Best in full sun, but satisfactory in part shade. Excellent as a cut flower and often grown in gardens for that reason as well as for its scent.

Popular for garden use are the *Dwarf Ten Week* and *Giant Imperial* strains. For cutting, the *Column* type is recommended.

Stock cannot tolerate heat in the early growing stages and must have a temperature of 65 degrees or less in order to produce a good set of buds. For best results, start seed indoors.

Sweet Pea Galaxy

Strawflower (Helichrysum)

Sunflower

Strawflower

Helichrysum bracteatum.
There are numerous annuals which can be included under the group name of strawflowers, but helichrysum is the most widely seen in gardens. A tender annual, it grows 1-1/2 to 2-1/2 feet tall.

The tall double mixture is the commonest type, producing a glistening display of colors, including crimson, salmon, rose, yellow and white. An excellent cut flower fresh from the garden. Colors are retained over a long period in dried arrangements.

To dry helichrysum, cut long stems, strip away the leaves, and tie the stems in bunches of separate colors. Wrap the bunches in a newspaper cone and hang upside down in a dark, dry place.

Seed does well direct-sown in the garden, or it can be started early indoors in areas where the growing season is very short.

Sunflower

Helianthus annuus. Tender annual, 3 to 7 ft., blooming mid-summer to fall in yellow and red. Takes heat, drought and poor soil.

The tall, large-flowered kinds, such as *Mammoth Russia,* are decorative as tall background flowers, and the meaty kernels can be saved to feed the birds in winter. This is the variety that wins in giant sunflower growing contests, some flower and seed heads reaching 24 in. or more across. *Sungold* has double flower heads up to 6 in. wide on 6 ft. tall plants. There is a dwarf version, *Teddy Bear,* just 2 ft. tall with 5-in. fully double flower heads.

The large, easy-to-handle seeds should be planted directly in the soil after danger of frost. For largest flower heads, a deep, fertile soil is necessary, although sunflowers do well in a wide variety of soils.

Sweet Pea

Lathyrus odoratus. Hardy annual, 8 in. to 6 ft. tall, flowering in late spring and early summer. Flowers in every color but yellow. Many sweet peas are delightfully scented. Older climbing varieties need support, new "bush-types" don't.

Sweet peas make superb cut flowers, and in the last 10 years breeders have made some major improvements. Recommended series: *Jet Set* and *Bijou. Jet Set* is a distinctly superior bush-type sweet pea and is available in fifteen hues. The large flowers are supported by long stems on short vines, producing a remarkable density of color. Like all sweet peas, *Jet Set* provides superb cut flowers. Among dwarf bush types, perhaps the most impressive is the *Bijou* series, growing just 12 in. high, but producing 5- to 7-in. stems with 4 or 5 flowers to each stem.

Where winters are mild, sweet peas can be sown outdoors in autumn, mulched, and relied upon to flower in early spring. However, in cold areas it is best to plant seed outdoors in early spring as soon as the ground can be worked. Starting seed indoors to get 6-in. healthy transplants is also a good method, especially where summers get hot, since sweet peas cannot tolerate heat and must be grown to flower as early in spring as possible. To hasten germination, soak the bullet-hard seeds for 24 hours in water. Soil for sweet peas should be fertile, well drained and in a sunny location.

Zinnia Whirligig

Vinca (Periwinkle)

Verbena Miss Susie

Verbena

Verbena hybrida. Half-hardy annual, 6 to 12 in. high, blooming midsummer to autumn in a wide range of colors including white, blue, red, pink and salmon, some with contrasting "eyes". Flowers grow in tight clusters on tough, spreading plants, which form a dense colorful carpet, withstanding heat and pool soil. Best in sun.

Verbena is useful for edging, ground covers and in the rock garden. Although mixtures such as *Ideal Florist, Rainbow* and *Sparkle* are popular, some individual colors have won All-America awards: *Amethyst* for its lovely lavender-blue flowers and *Blaze* for its dazzling bright scarlet ones.

Sow seed directly in the garden after danger of frost or start indoors to get healthy transplants.

Vinca

Catharanthus rosea; formerly *Vinca Rosea* (Madagascar-periwinkle). Tender annual, 4 to 15 in. tall, blooming midsummer to autumn. Best in sun, but thrives in light shade. Flowers are white, shades of rose and pink, some with a contrasting "eye". Leaves are dark glossy green, stems fleshy. Some varieties grow upright, but the most popular ones are spreaders.

Fine planted around the base of a tree, providing it doesn't have a dense canopy. Also good as a border plant, edging, ground cover, and in containers. Seems insect- and disease-free. *Polka Dot,* an All-America winner, has white flowers with red centers. Very showy, especially in light shade.

Start seeds indoors for early bloom or purchase young plants for the garden after danger of frost has passed.

Zinnia

Zinnia elegans. Tender annual, 6 in. to 3-1/2 ft. tall, blooming from midsummer to autumn. Brightly colored flowers in various shapes, sizes and hues, including white, yellow, pink, red and orange. Garden uses are similar to marigold. A choice cut flower.

Giant cactus-flowered types, with blooms up to 6 in. or more, are the most popular. They have quilled, ruffled petals. Next in popularity among the giants are dahlia-flowered types, with wide flat petals forming a rounded flower head up to 5 in. across. Giant tetraploid varieties, of which *State Fair Mixture* is a good example, have even larger blooms than the dahlia-flowered type. They are also more disease-resistant.

Almost as popular are the dwarfs. Among these is *Thumbelina,* a gold medal All-America winner growing no taller than 8 in. It blooms when only 3 in. tall.

Peter Pan types, F1 hybrids, are a breeding achievement. They grow to a foot and have dahlia-type flowers up to 3 in. across. Plants are bushy and compact. Best in mass plantings. Especially recommended.

Easy and dependable from seed sown directly in the garden. May also be started indoors or young plants can be purchased in spring.

Good Companions in a Flower Bed

Above *Four popular, easy-to-grow flowering annuals create a stunning island bed. White alyssum forms a dense edging with multiflora petunias, Rose Joy, providing intermediate height, while taller snapdragons and American marigolds add additional color and interest.*

Above Yellow Rainbow *coleus (background),* Scarletta *hybrid wax begonias (intermediate height) and variegated pepper* (capsium variegata), *used as an edging, create this distinctive border with* Scarlet Ruffles *zinnia at the far end.*

Below Harvest Moon, *dwarf French marigolds (foreground) and* Purity *dahlia-flowered hybrid zinnias create a colorful border with yellow double-flowered rudbeckias in the background.*

Above *Pink and blue predominate to make this eyecatching border, using vinca, multiflora petunias, snapdragons, ageratum and cleome (spider plant).*

Above *Crimson impatiens, blue grandiflora petunias, dusty miller and nicotiana (extreme left) combine to make a colorful corner around evergreens.*

Below *In the foreground hybrid bicolored dianthus creates a spectacular contrast to dwarf* Floral Carpet *snapdragons with geraniums, calendulas and wax begonias in strategically placed containers.*

Above *This double-tiered curving bed features two of the most colorful, long lasting annuals — petite marigolds in a mixture and a bold single color of pink flowered, bronze-foliaged hybrid wax begonias.*

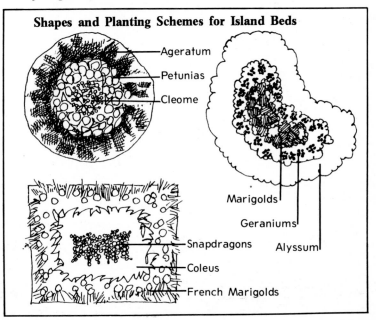

Shapes and Planting Schemes for Island Beds

Ageratum
Petunias
Cleome

Marigolds
Geraniums
Alyssum

Snapdragons
Coleus
French Marigolds

This old lithograph print is taken from a 1908 seed catalog. Pansies are one of the most effective flowers for pressed flower plaques.

Plant a Patch of Pansies

Promise yourself a beautiful massed bed of pansies by making preparations in summer to avoid the cost of buying ready-grown plants. To have blooming pansies early in the year, seed should be sown in July or August so that seedlings — transplanted in the fall — will reach an almost ready-to-bloom stage before winter sets in and holds them back, ready to burst forth into glorious bloom at the first sign of spring.

It takes 6 weeks during warm weather for seed to grow into sizeable plants for transplanting, then another 5 weeks until they are large enough to go through the winter.

Sow seed in a cold frame or outdoors in a shaded seed bed. The soil must be fairly rich. Dig in liberal quantities of compost or leaf mold and peat. The seed is very fine — a pinch will go a long way and should be covered with not more than 1/8 inch of fine soil. Keep moist and allow 8 to 10 days for germination. In September, when the seedlings have reached a good size, they can be transferred to their permanent locations, spaced 6 to 9 inches apart.

In northern areas a mulch of straw, peat or finely shredded leaves will help protect them during winter. Heavy freezing will not injure pansies, but alternate freezings and thawings will, so mulching is a wise precaution. When the warm spring weather begins, remove the mulch and watch the plants burst into life, unfolding their friendly faces even before the daffodils appear. If you keep faded flowers picked, the pansies will bloom well into summer.

There are dozens of different varieties to choose from, depending on your preference. Some have clear faces, other are blotched. A new race of hybrids called *Majestic Giants*, from Japan, produces the largest flowers of all in colors ranging from white and yellow to red, blue and purple, all beautifully blotched. Other good hybrids are *Sunny Boy*, a golden yellow with distinctive black blotch, and *Imperial Blue*, the most heat resistant pansy ever introduced, and winner of an All-America award.

Green Grow the Flowers

Green is one of the least common colors in the flower kingdom, and yet is one of the most popular colors with flower gardeners. Green as a color is uncommon because most flowers must contrast with green foliage in order to catch the attention of insects for pollination. For this reason blue is an uncommon color because blue is the color of the sky. Black is almost non-existent, although some scabiosa and pansies are almost black. White, yellow and red are most common as flower colors.

Gardeners like green flowers mainly because of their decorative value indoors. The two most famous garden flowers with green coloring are Bells of Ireland, growing long, slender flower spikes surrounded by cup-shaped flower custers, and *Envy* zinnia, a lime green dahlia-flowered zinnia. Both are extremely easy to grow.

Bells of Ireland are best sown directly into the ground after all danger of frost in an open, sunny position. *Envy* zinnia likes the same. Both will mature in mid-summer to help create stunning flower arrangements. Other unusual green flowers are *Green Woodpecker*, a fine gladiolus, and *Limelight*, a pale green nicotiana.

Zinnia Envy, *one of the most popular of all "green" flowers*

All of the flowers in this picture — tulips and pansies — are edible.

Day lily May Hall looks good enough to eat — and she is.

Flowers for Food

There are numerous plants with edible flowers, many of them quite common. Here are some of the most popular:

Marigold. Marigold petals — particularly the large deep orange kinds like Hawaii — may eventually replace saffron as a flavoring and food coloring. Saffron, processed from the golden-yellow centers of crocus flowers, is costly and has to be imported from remote areas of the world. Yet marigold petals are just as useful, especially in flavoring scrambled eggs and adding color to rice dishes.

Chrysanthemum. Add these as a garnish to many kinds of vegetable side dishes.

Nasturtium. All of the nasturtium plant is good to eat — the leaves, the stems, the seeds (as capers) and the flowers. The orange-red flowers especially are good to add color and flavor to salads, imparting a flavor similar to garden cress.

Tulips, Hollyhocks and Gladiolus. Yellow, red and purple tulips make excellent containers for cream cheese, caviar and dips. The cup-shaped kinds are best for this purpose. Similarly, hollyhocks and gladiolus flowers can be used to good effect. Gladiolus petals have a flavor similar to lettuce, and the deep red varieties are particularly good to use because of the pleasing color contrast with leafy green vegetables.

Day lilies and Squash. The blossoms of these two flowers are prized by the Orientals, particularly when the blossoms are dipped in batter and fried. Also, they can be added to salads for a delicate flavor — not unlike chestnuts in the case of day lilies.

Yucca. The yucca flower has a mild asparagus flavor. They are good in salads, eaten raw or creamed.

Pansies. Although pansies have little or no flavor, they are edible, and the colorful flower faces are interesting to use whole in certain gelatin desserts where you can see through the clear gelatin to the bright cheerful flowers.

Carnations. The petals of the carnation have a spicy taste, with a flavor like cloves or cinnamon, and are useful as a substitute for both.

Roses and Violets. These two flowers have the widest use of all edible flowers. Both can be candied and converted into fragrant, colorful waters. Violets are known to be high in vitamin C — the leaves are also edible in salads — and the rose lends itself to syrups, icings, puddings, fruit salads, jams, omelets, pancakes and crab or lobster salad.

One word of caution, however, before you rush off to try your hand at cooking with flowers. ALWAYS WASH ALL FLOWERS THOROUGHLY BUT GENTLY. It is best to use flowers from *your own garden* that you know have not been sprayed with harmful chemicals. Never use flowers from a florist or grower, since these may have heavy applications of toxic elements on them.

Flowers for Dried Arrangements

Strawflowers, or helichrysum, are favorite flowers for dried arrangements.

Although it's possible to dry virtually every kind of flower, some are distinctly easier than others and retain their color longer.

Before starting to dry flowers, it's best to realize that they fit into two basic groups. First are the so-called everlasting flowers which require minimum trouble — simple air-drying. Then there are those which require the help of drying agents or preservatives.

In the first group, the most widely-grown "everlasting" flowers are helichrysum, helipterum (*acroclinium*), honesty, gomphrena (globe amaranth), ornamental grasses, such as Job's Tears, and statice. All these flowers have a strawy or parchment-like texture, which makes them very easy to dry and gives them a sturdiness that allows them to keep a long time. These are the easiest of all to start with.

Next in order of popularity are Bells of Ireland, ornamental gourds, gypsophila and crested cockscomb. Hang these to dry, heads down in a cool, dark ventilated place. Gourds are ready when you hear the seeds rattle inside, after which they can be varnished.

By using a drying agent, it is possible to dry a wider range of flowers, such as pansies, marigolds and zinnias. As a general rule, the color and form of a dried flower depends on how fast you can remove all the moisture and prevent exposure to light during drying. An absorbant powder is the most efficient kind of drying agent, such as Silica Gel.

Cut flowers on a dry day at the peak of freshness, choosing those with crisp clean petals. Place the flowers face down and stem up in a bowl with the drying agent. Flowers on spikes should be placed horizontally. Add more drying agent around the petals, filling in every nook and cranny, until the flower is completely buried.

Drying time will depend on the flower, but the more popular kinds such as pansies, cornflowers, cosmos, dahlias, shasta daisies, marigolds and zinnias will take 4 to 6 days.

Pressing flowers is also a great pastime. This is done by sandwiching the flowers between blotting paper, then inserting them between the pages of a heavy book for up to a week until dry. Pansies are especially good to start with, pressing them face down, then mounting them on card, decorated with pressed fern leaves.

Easiest Flowers to Dry by Air-Drying

Bells of Ireland
Celosia, Crested
Gomphrena
Gourds, Ornamental
Grass, Ornamental
Gypsophila
Helichrysum
Honesty
Statice

Easiest Flowers to Dry in Drying Agent

Aster, China
Chrysanthemum
Cornflower
Cosmos
Daffodil (especially small-cupped)
Dahlia
Daisy, Shasta
Larkspur
Liatris
Marigold
Pansy (especially bold colors)
Peony
Queen Anne's Lace
Rose (before fully open)
Rudbeckia
Sweet Pea
Tulip (open petals flat for drying)
Zinnia (especially dahlia-flowered)

How to Grow Perennials

Perennials are garden plants that live from year to year, producing ornamental flowers or foliage. Their roots live in the soil over winter, with varying degrees of cold tolerance (hardiness), and the tops usually die back.

Some flowers classified as perennials are really biennials. After flowering the second season, the plants are too weak to continue. Honesty, sweet william and foxgloves are examples of biennials, although biennials generally have the ability to self-seed readily, and therefore appear to be perennials.

Some perennials can be treated as annuals to flower the first year if seed is sown early. Gloriosa daises, dianthus and hardy hibiscus are good examples. In southern and Pacific coast areas, perennials and biennials are best treated as annuals. If planted in the fall, they grow during cool weather, bloom the following spring, and then die.

Soil Preparation

Proper soil preparation is more important for perennials than it is for annuals. Most need a deeply worked fertile soil to maintain vigorous growth.

Good perennial beds need good drainage and a soil with good "tilth" to a depth of at least 1-1/2 feet. Tilth describes the physical condition of the soil, and a good tilth lets roots penetrate freely, allowing for plant nutrients to be readily absorbed by the roots. Clay or sandy soils do not have good tilth, and can be improved by the addition of well-decomposed organic matter. The best fertilizer to use for perennial beds is a *slow release*, or *timed released*, flower fertilizer in dry granular form, which can be sprinkled on the soil by hand at planting time or in the spring as a booster application. Ground with poor drainage can be made suitable for perennials by creating a raised bed from railroad ties on a layer of crushed stones.

Seeds or Plants

Most perennials are available as transplants from nurseries and garden centers in spring, or they can be grown from seed direct-sown into the garden where the plants are to grow or in specially prepared seed beds in a semishaded area which does not dry out quickly. Midsummer is the best time to start plants because it allows perennials to reach good size before winter dormancy.

Then the higher temperatures and longer days of spring boost them into glorious bloom.

Plant Division

Some perennials, such as flowering bulbs, bearded iris, garden lilies and peonies, take too long to mature from seed and are better grown from healthy root divisions or bulbs. It's possible to make root divisions from established plants by dividing up thick clumps.

Divide mature clumps of perennials after 3 years. This usually can be done in spring or fall.

Divide clumps into sections of 3 to 5 shoots each. Smaller divisions with only 1 or 2 sprouts will take longer to bloom.

Stem Cuttings

Many perennials can be increased by stem cuttings. Dianthus, candytuft, geraniums, carnations, baby's breath and phlox are good examples. After they have finished blooming, select 4 to 6 inch-long side shoots of healthy plants. Trim the cutting just below a leaf joint and remove the leaves from the part that will be below the soil line. Dip each cutting into a hormone root stimulant and insert it into a peat pot filled with a soil mix of 2 parts sand, 1 part garden loam and 1 part peat moss. Then place the cuttings in a propagator or frame in a shaded location. Cover the propagator with glass or plastic; this will keep them moist and maintain an even soil temperature of at least 50 degrees. After several weeks, gently tug each cutting to see if it has rooted.

Perennials That Act Like Annuals

Southern Belle, a new giant hybrid hibiscus, acts like an annual and is classified a perennial. In other words, it will bloom the first year from seed, and then it will keep coming back year after year.

For blooms the first year, seed is best started indoors at room temperature, then transplanted to the garden after danger of frost. Flowers will bloom from August until frost. To ensure a repeat performance the next year, the old stems should be cut back and the roots protected with a layer of mulch.

In the world of ornamental flowers, there are many other varieties like *Southern Belle* hibiscus which are really perennials, but can be grown as annuals to flower the first year — if seed is started early. The secret is to get good-size plants for setting out into the garden as soon as the soil warms up.

Delphiniums are another good example. Seed started 8 weeks before planting outside will produce foot-high plants capable of flowering the first year. Gloriosa daisies, dianthus and charm chrysanthemums can be treated the same way, and so can the newer varieties of hollyhocks, such as *Summer Carnival*. Blue salvia will also flower the first year from an early sowing.

How to Divide Perennials

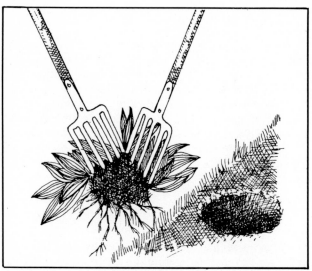

1. Thick perennial clumps may need separating into smaller clumps by using garden forks to make divisions.

2. Separate smaller clumps by hand, ensuring each clump has a healthy growing crown and roots.

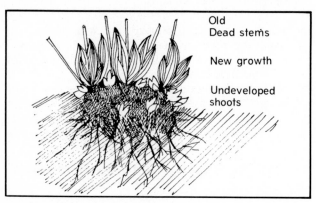

Old
Dead stems

New growth

Undeveloped
shoots

3. In the ground, a typical perennial clump will look like this — with the thick root ball hollow in the middle. Sometimes new growth is not as obvious as shown here, especially in fall after frost.

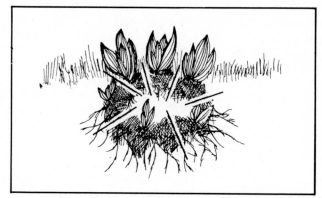

4. Lift clump with fork or spade. Wash away large clumps of soil. Pull and separate into divisions, each division containing new growth or buds, old stems and a root system. Smallest divisions with insignificant crown or roots can be discarded or planted together.

Hints on Staking

Bushy, upright perennials, such as peonies, and clumps of tall-stemmed perennials, such as garden lilies, will need staking to keep them neat and tidy. Best way to do this is with fishing line tied to bamboo stakes. With heavier flower spikes like delphiniums, an individual stake with twist-ties to secure the stem may be necessary.

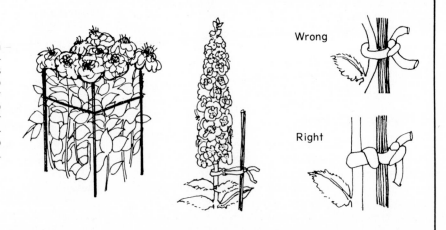

Wrong

Right

How to Multiply Perennials from Cuttings

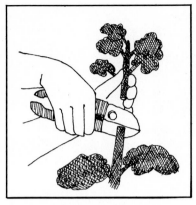

1. Cut off a 5-inch-long side shoot.

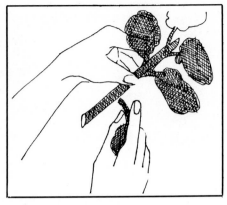

2. Remove lower leaves.

3. Dip end in rooting hormone.

4. Set firmly in soil mix.

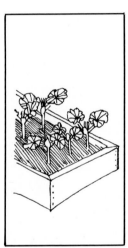
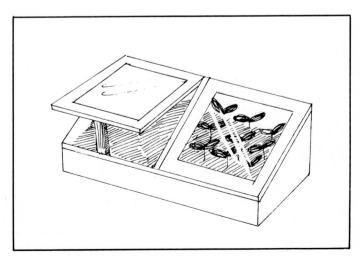

5. Place cuttings in propagator, made from seed flat, with plastic cover.

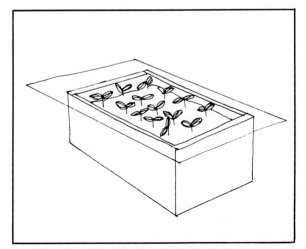

6. Alternatively, use deep box covered with glass.

7. Set out in cold frames during winter.

Ajuga

Alyssum saxatile

Achillea Gold Plate

Anchusa

Perennials for Stunning Borders

The following listing of perennials features the most useful and readily available kinds. Some, like rudbeckias and delphiniums, are easy to grow from seed, while others, like iris and peonies, are best planted from root divisions or rooted cuttings available through mail-order catalogs, from garden centers or by trading with neighbors. Recommendations for each type of propagation are given, as well as information about whether the perennial is hardy or tender.

Some biennials are included in the list, and these are identified.

Achillea
Achillea filipendulina (Yarrow). Hardy perennial, 2 ft. high, blooming from June to September, producing flat panicles of tight yellow flower clusters. Makes a good display flower for a sunny perennial border. Also good as a long-lasting cut flower.

Easily grown from seed, which germinates in 10 days from sowing outside in spring, summer or fall. Plants of named varieties are also readily available from nurseries and by propagation from cuttings or root division in spring or fall.

When plants have ceased flowering, cut the shoots back. Since well-established plants grow vigorously, it is best to lift roots, divide and replant every third year, spacing 36 in. apart.

The most desirable yellow varieties are *Gold Plate* and *Coronation Gold*. Other good varieties are *Fire King* (*Achillea Millefolium*), a rosy red with cream centers; and *The Pearl* (*Achillea Ptarmica*), growing clusters of small, white, pompon-like flowers. All are best used sparingly as an accent in borders.

Ajuga
Ajuga genevensis (Blue Bugle). Hardy perennial, 6 in. high, useful as a fast-spreading ground cover, in sun or shade. Tolerates a wide range of soil conditions, including poor dry soil. Grows colorful rosettes of leaves in green or bronze with masses of deep blue flower spikes in early spring.

Spreads by runners and is best planted in spring or fall from roots spaced 6 in. apart. Stays evergreen all year.

Alyssum
Alyssum saxatile (Gold Dust). Hardy perennial, 9 to 12 in. high, creating a dense mound of golden-yellow flowers in early spring. Excellent for rock gardens and crevices of dry walls or as an edging to borders of spring-flowering bulbs. Thrives in a sunny location, even in dry soil, but gives its best show in slightly sandy soil.

Easily grown from seed planted outdoors in spring or from nursery-bought plants spaced 6 in. apart. Seed germinates in 5 days. This is the most valuable rock plant you can grow, since no other rock garden subject can match it for sheer brilliance. Combines especially well with tulips and forget-me-nots.

Anchusa
Anchusa italica. Hardy perennial, 4 to 5 ft. tall, growing long flower stems covered with hundreds of blue flowers resembling forget-me-nots, in late spring and early summer. Useful in perennial borders, especially as a background plant, and good as a cut flower.

Easily grown from seed sown outdoors anytime from May to September in a sunny position, spacing 12 in. apart. Seed germinates in 20 days, aided by chilling in a refrigerator for 7 days.

Annual forms of anchusa are also available. (See section on Annuals).

Anemone
There are many kinds of anemones, some hardy and others tender. Most popular among the hardy anemones are

Armeria (Sea Pinks)   *Artemesia Silver Mound*   *Anemone De Caen*

Anemone Pulsatilla (Pasque flower), producing large purple flowers in early spring and *Anemone blanda*, (Grecian windflower) grown from bulbs and creating a carpet of starry deep blue flowers with yellow centers.

The anemone everyone wants to grow, however, is not reliably hardy north of Washington D.C., and that is *Anemone coronaria*, of which the giant French strain called De Caen is the most outstanding example. The rich color mixture includes brilliant red and blue, with black, powdery centers. These are the kinds widely used by florists, and popular as a pot plant grown indoors.

Where winters are mild or where a sheltered bed or cold frame is available, *Anemone coronaria* can be grown from bulbs planted 3 in. deep and at least 6 in. apart, in a fertile sandy soil enriched with organic matter. Then mulch the beds to a depth of 6 in. with straw or shredded leaves. Alternatively, buy bulbs in spring and treat as an annual, planting them in the soil after danger of frost and lifting them in fall.

Anthemis

Anthemis tinctoria (Chamomile). Hardy perennial, 2 ft. high, with yellow daisy-like flowers appearing from late spring to frost. The finely cut foliage is highly ornamental and slightly aromatic. Thrives in a wide range of soil conditions, but does especially well in dry, sandy soil and rock gardens.

Makes an excellent cut flower and grows easily from seed sown directly into the garden after all danger of frost.

Arabis

Arabis alpina (Rock Cress). Hardy perennial, 8 to 12 in. high, growing masses of tiny pink or white flowers in such profusion that they create a low spreading plant excellent for rock gardens and crevices in dry walls. Reaches peak bloom in early spring, preferring a slightly shaded location.

Start plants from seed anytime from May to Septemer or purchase nursery-grown plants, spacing 12 in. apart. Seeds germinate in 5 days.

Armeria

Armeria alpina (Sea Pinks). Hardy perennial, 18 to 24 in. high, blooming in spring. Useful in rock gardens and also as a ground cover on dry sunny slopes. The mound-shaped plants form neat evergreen tufts, while the globular pink flowers grow on stems long enough for cutting and dense enough to create a carpet of color.

Start seed anytime from May to September in sandy soil or buy young plants, spacing them 12 in. apart. Established plants can be divided by root division in spring or fall. Seeds germinate in 10 days.

Artemesia

Artemisia Stelleriana. Hardy perennial, 2 ft. high, growing as a mound of silver-blue foliage suitable for borders and rock gardens. Although it does produce panicles of yellow and white flowers, its silky, silvery blue foliage is the reason to grow it.

Silver Mound is probably the most handsome named variety, growing to 12 in. high, and exquisite when used as an edging along walks. Prefers a warm, sunny location and is easily grown from seed planted from late spring to late summer or from young nursery-bought plants, spaced 12 in. apart.

Aster, Hardy

Aster alpinus. Hardy perennial, 1 to 2 ft. high, in white and shades of blue, with golden-yellow centers. Valuable for rock gardens and perennial borders, blooming in June. Easily grown from seed planted outdoors in spring in a sunny location.

Michaelmas daisies, a common name to describe a number of fall blooming perennial asters, make an exquisite display. The white, red and blue flowers almost smother the plants and provide a density of color few other plants can match at that time of year. Full sun and moist soil are their chief requirements, although they will tolerate a wide range of soil conditions.

37

Astilbe Deutschland   Canterbury Bells   Candytuft

Astilbe

Astilbe japonica (Spiraea). Hardy perennial, 2-1/2 to 3 feet high, creating bushy clumps with beautiful feathery flower spikes in white, pink and red during midsummer, thriving in full sun or semishade.

Astilbe enjoys a deep, fertile, moist soil, especially if it contains leaf mold or well-decomposed animal manure. Makes a good cut flower and is easily grown from root divisions, planted in early spring or fall, spaced 24 in. apart. Started from seed in early spring, germination takes 14 to 21 days.

Aubretia

Aubretia deltoidea graecea (Rainbow Rock Cress). Hardy perennial, 6 in. high, used extensively in rock gardens and dry walls. A dwarf spreading plant, its purple flowers appear in early spring.

Plant seed outdoors anytime from spring to September in light shade or indoors in March at no more than 60 degree soil temperature, since higher temperatures discourage germination, which normally takes up to 20 days. Well established plants can be divided in late summer and then planted 12 in. apart.

Candytuft

Iberis sempervirens. Hardy perennial, 10 in. high, flowering in June in white or pink. Does well in dry places, such as rock gardens, and as an edging or ground cover in beds and borders. Annual varieties are also available. Plant 6 to 8 in. apart.

To grow the perennial kind, sow seeds in spring or fall in a sunny location. Shear flowers as they fade to promote branching plants.

Canterbury Bells

Campanula Medium. Hardy biennial, 2 to 2-1/2 feet high, producing flower stems packed with cup-shaped flowers in white, rose and blue. Creates a handsome display plant in June. Likes partial shade and can be propagated from root divisions every other year.

Sow seed outdoors in June or July, or buy nursery-grown transplants for setting out in May or June, spaced 20 in. apart.

Related to Canterbury Bells is *Campanula carpatica,* a useful hardy perennial producing masses of tapering spikes with violet-blue flowers in June.

Carnation

Dianthus Caryophyllus. Tender perennial, some varieties capable of being grown as annuals to flower the first year from seed. Grow 18 to 24 in. high, in a wide color range that includes white, yellow, red, purple and striped bicolors. Blooms best in late summer and early fall when cool sunny weather sets in. Excellent for borders and as a cut flower, possessing a fragrance similar to cloves.

Sow seed of annual varieties indoors about February 15, germinating the seed at 55 to 65 degree soil temperature, chilling seeds in a refrigerator for 7 days to break dormancy. Alternatively sow outside after danger of frost and transplant to 8 in. apart for blooms in late summer and fall.

Perennial varieties can be sown indoors November 1st, germinating at 55 to 60 degree soil temperature for 20 days and hardening-off in a cold frame before setting plants out into flowering positions 4 weeks before the last frost date. In mild areas seed can be sown outdoors in June for flowers the following year. In northern areas they will not survive the winter unless planted close to the house in a sheltered place and heavily mulched. In northern areas it's best to pot up a number of choice plants and hold them in a cold frame for winter protection.

Flowering-size plants are readily available from local nurseries in spring, and these can be spaced 12 in. apart when planted. Carnations are also easily propagated by "layering," which involves pegging a stem into the soil, allowing it to take root, and then transplanting it to a favored location or to a pot. They enjoy a light, fertile soil, enriched with garden compost or well-decayed animal manure.

Annual varieties have been enhanced by a new race of dwarf carnations, growing just 12 in. tall. The best of these is a scarlet

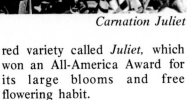
Carnation Juliet

Cerastium

Chrysanthemum Grandchild

red variety called *Juliet,* which won an All-America Award for its large blooms and free flowering habit.

Centaurea

Centaurea montana. Hardy perennial 2 ft. high, blooming from June to September. The clear blue flowers resemble cornflowers, but they are much larger — up to 3 in. across.

Useful in borders and as a cut flower, they are easy to grow from seed planted outside in spring about 2 weeks before the last expected frost date. Indoors, seed germinates best at 60 degree soil temperature for 30 days in total darkness. Space plants 16 in. apart and remove dead flowers to prolong the blooming period.

Cerastium

Cerastium tomentosum (Snow in Summer). Hardy perennial, 6 in. high, forming a dense low growing mass of brilliant white flowers. Used extensively in rock gardens, dry walls and as a ground cover. Blooms in May and June, thriving in dry sunny locations.

The silvery-white woolly foliage is equally decorative when the plants are not in bloom. Easy to grow from seeds sown outdoors in May, germinating best at 65 degree soil temperature in 30 days. Nursery-grown plants are also widely available in spring. Space 8 in. apart.

Chinese Lanterns

Physalis Alkegengi. Hardy perennial, 2 ft. high, grown for its decorative orange-red, lantern-shaped seed pods, which mature in fall of the second year. In fresh flower arrangements, they will keep for several weeks, and they are easily dried for longer lasting dried flower arrangements.

Thrives in a wide range of garden soils in a sunny location. Easily grown from seed, and spreads by underground stems. The simplest method of propagation is to divide plants into rooted sections and replant in early spring spaced 15 in. apart. Raised from seed, they can be direct-sown into the garden after danger of frost in spring.

Chrysanthemums, Border

Hardy chrysanthemums are indispensable for late summer and fall color. Nothing among flowering perennials will provide the color range equal to chrysanthemums from fall onwards.

The huge globular "florist" chrysanthemums really have no place in the perennial border. They need to be propagated carefully each year indoors in a greenhouse and grown on single stems.

For the most beautiful flower beds and borders, it is the dwarf "cushion" mums, such as the Korean hybrids, which are more practical. The official classification of outdoor mums is rather complex, but basically there are the *decoratives,* growing the largest flowers and some with bold incurving petals, *pompons,* forming compact ball-shaped blooms, *spoons,* with curled petals, and *spiders,* having long, narrow petals.

Chrysanthemums are popularly grown from rooted cuttings available from specialist mail-order nurseries in spring, or as pot plants in bud for transplanting in fall. However, both the large-flowered *japonicum* chrysanthemums, and the small-flowered Korean hybrids are easily grown from seeds sown in March and transplanted outdoors in May, for flowering in fall.

The two most successful varieties grown from seed are *Autumn Glory,* a glorious all-color mixture of single and semi-double flowers in such profusion they completely hide the foliage, and *Golden Dream,* a deep yellow with incredible vigor and uniformity, growing mounds of densely packed daisy-like flowers spreading 2 ft. across.

Chrysanthemums like a sunny position, fertile soil, and watering during dry spells. They are readily increased by root division made in spring or fall and by cuttings started in February or March.

To get a full cushion effect, it is most important to pinch off the lead shoot when the plants are 4 in. high. This will encourage side shoots and a fuller plant.

Columbine McKana Giant   *Shasta Daisy*   *Coreopsis*

Columbine

Aquilegia hybrida. These hardy perennials have one of the most unusual flower forms of all home garden plants. The vigorous, bushy plants produce hundreds of stems topped by graceful flowers made up of three distinct portions — a group of tubular petals at the middle, surrounded by 5 wide flat petals, all ending in a long arching spur.

Largest-flowered variety of all is *McKana Giants,* bred by an amateur gardener called McKana. They were the first perennial ever to win an All-America award and the first All-America winner ever to be awarded to a new flower bred by an amateur. Growing 2 to 3 ft. high, individual flowers measure up to 2 in. across, in a range of pastel colors including white, cream, yellow, pink, red, blue.

Best planted in a perennial border with foxgloves and delphiniums, there are also dwarf varieties suitable for growing in small spaces, especially in rock gardens.

Seed sown early indoors in February will generally produce transplants large enough to flower the first season when transferred to the garden after the last frost date. Alternatively, seed can be sown directly into the garden outdoors in May or June to produce hardy plants that will survive the winter and bloom early the following year.

Individual stems of the tall varieties are long enough to be cut and make one of the most appealing flower arrangements

Coreopsis

Coreopsis grandiflora. Hardy perennial, 2 to 3 ft. high, growing clear yellow single and double flowers from May until fall.

Showy in the garden as a display plant and excellent for cutting, it likes a sunny location and will resist drought. Thrives on neglect, and doesn't mind crowding.

Easily grown from seed sown outdoors from April to June or inside, germinating seed at 75 degree soil temperature for 20 days. Also propagates from root divisions made in early spring or fall, spacing plants 12 in. apart.

Daisy, English

Bellis perennis. Hardy annual, 6 in. high, used in beds, borders and especially rock gardens during cool weather of early spring and fall. Likes cool, moist, well-drained soil. The compact plants form tight rosettes of leaves, with double flowers in white, crimson and pink.

Easily grown from seed sown in midsummer and treated like pansies. Seeds need light for successful germination and should be lightly pressed into the soil without covering.

Daisy, Shasta

Chrysanthemum maximum. Hardy perennial, 2 to 3 ft. high, used extensively in sunny and semishaded perennial borders where it makes a magnificent display and provides a source of lovely cut flowers for dazzling white indoor arrangements.

The white-petalled flowers have yellow "ox-eye" centers and bloom in June and July, each bloom measuring 3 to 7 in. across, depending on variety. Both single- and double-flowered kinds are available. Plant seed anytime from spring to September outdoors, pressing seed lightly into the soil, but do not cover, since the seeds need light to germinate reliably.

Day lilies

Hemerocallis hybrids. Day lilies have a reputation for being the most undemanding of all hardy perennials, thriving on neglect in soils that few other flowers can tolerate. Although the flowers themselves last only a day, there are sufficient numbers on each stem to ensure a succession of bloom for several weeks during July and August.

Plants grow 4 ft. high, creating a dense growth of slender, arching, sword-shaped leaves which remain ornamental all through the growing season. Colors range from pale yellow to deep maroon with the orange and deep yellows providing the most spectacular displays.

Full sun, semishade, moist soil and dry soil — all these conditions favor day lilies. Only heavily waterlogged soil or dense shade will deter them.

The trumpet-shaped flowers open at dawn and close at dusk, and they are edible. In the Orient they are considered a delicacy — eaten raw or served as appetizers dipped in batter and fried.

Echinops

Delphinium Pacific Giant

Day Lily

Dianthus alpinus

Planting of day lily roots can be done anytime, although fall is the favored period, setting them 1 in. below the soil line. For stunning all-around display of day lilies nothing quite beats a yellow, such as *Cartwheels,* a peach, such as *Sea Gold,* and a deep red, such as *War Eagle.* Also worth space in every perennial border is the fragrant, early-flowering lemon-yellow day lily known as *Hemerocallis citrina,* seen in late May and early June.

Easily grown from seed started indoors March 1st at 70 degree soil temperature for 20 days. Plants mature in 16 months from seed.

Delphiniums

Delphinium elatum. Delphiniums are one of the most popular hardy perennials grown from seed, second only to rudbeckias or gloriosa daisies. These tall, stately plants, growing up to 5 ft. tall, can be treated as annuals to flower the first year, providing seed is sown early indoors in peat pellets about the same time as tomato seeds to get strong healthy transplants. Seed can also be sown outdoors in a seed bed after danger of frost or in late summer for blooms the next year.

Among the most popular classes are the Pacific Giants, growing tall heavy flower spikes, crowded with large well-spaced blooms ranging in color from sky-blue and deep blue to white and pink. Most popular of all are the blues, since blue is not a common color in the flower garden.

Delphiniums bloom early in the year when nights are cool and generally die down when summer heat turns on. Often they can be cut back like snapdragons, fed a booster fertilizer, and encouraged to send up additional spikes during the cooler days of fall.

At the center of each delphinium bloom is a ring of smaller petals often referred to as a "bee" and usually in a contrasting color. In addition to the tall types, there are also dwarf varieties, notably *Connecticut Yankees,* which will bloom reliably from seed the first year even from an outdoor sowing.

Best germination of seed is assured with delphiniums if the seed is pre-chilled in a refrigerator for 24 hours, and sown in a fine soil mixture or peat pellet at average temperatures of 60 degrees.

Good companion plants with delphiniums are foxgloves, which bloom at the same time in early summer and have a similar tall tapering habit.

Dianthus

Dianthus alpinus, Dianthus deltoides, Dianthus plumarius (Pinks). Hardy perennials invaluable for rock gardens, dry walls and sunny borders. Growing 12 in. high and blooming in May, they do best in stony soils that contain lime and should not be confused with the annual kind, *Dianthus chinensis.* (See section on annuals.)

The cottage pinks (or *Dianthus plumarius*) have fragrant flowers in both double and single forms in shades of red, white and pink. The maiden pinks (*Dianthus deltoides*) are characterized by red or pink blooms with a contrasting eye of deeper color, forming a dense mass of low-growing leaves and flowers effective as a ground cover or trailing plant. Alpine pinks (*Dianthus alpinus*) are exquisite planted as an edging to perennial borders, among stepping stones, or forming clumps of color on dry walls.

Nursery-grown plants are readily available in spring. Or start plants from seed anytime from spring to September in a sunny place, spacing plants 12 in. apart. Seed germinates in 5 days.

Echinops

Echinops Ritro (Globe Thistle). Hardy perennial, 4 ft. high, growing globular blue flower heads on long slender stems bearing prickly foliage. The flower heads change to metallic blue, prickly seed heads and are valued by flower arrangers for adding dramatic effect to indoor arrangements and dried flower centerpieces.

Flowers in midsummer but stays ornamental into fall, enjoying a wide range of soils.

Easily grown from seeds sown outdoors in April or May, by root divisions made in fall or early spring, or by root cuttings taken in fall or winter and raised in a cold frame.

Gaillardia

Helianthemum

Helianthus

Gaillardia

Gaillardia grandiflora. Hardy biennial, 30 in. high, and flowering in midsummer with daisy-like blooms which are generally yellow with maroon centers.

Likes sun, tolerates dry soil, and is easily grown from seed sown directly into the garden from April to September. Seed germinates best in total darkness after 20 days at 80 degree soil temperature, after which it needs full sun. Annual forms are also popular. (See section on annuals.)

Geum

Geum chiloense. Hardy perennial, 2 ft. high, blooming over long periods from spring to fall. Double flowers resemble tiny peonies, in scarlet and golden yellow. Good for garden display and as a cut flower.

Grows well in average soil and a sunny location. Easily grown from seed sown outdoors in May or started indoors by mid-February, germinating in 25 days at 70 degree soil temperature. Best planted in groups of 3 spaced 12 in. apart in the perennial border. Needs mulching in northern areas for complete winter protection.

Gypsophila

Gypsophila paniculata (Baby's Breath). Hardy perennial, 2 to 3 ft. high, with billowing, airy sprays of double pink and white flowers, blooming from ' early

summer to fall. The dainty flowers appear in such profusion they create the appearance of a mist when viewed from a distance. Thrives in a well-drained soil and full sun. Valuable as a cut flower and for dried arrangements.

Easily grown from seed started indoors or sown directly into the garden from spring to September, germinating in 10 days. Root divisions can be planted in fall or early spring, spaced 24 in. apart. Excellent for rock gardens.

Helianthemum

Helianthemum mutabile (Rock Rose). Hardy perennial, growing 1 ft. high dwarf evergreen plants covered with hundreds of rose, pink, yellow or white flowers in May or June. Grows well in dry, sunny locations, especially rock gardens and dry walls.

Easily grown from seed started indoors or sown directly into the garden from spring to September. Germination takes 5 days, and plants should be spaced 15 in. apart.

Helianthus

Helianthus decapetalus (Perennial Sunflower). Although the name helianthus is commonly used to describe the tall giant-flowered annual sunflower widely grown for its edible seeds, there is a large group of perennial sunflowers useful in the perennial border, the best of which is

probably *decapetalus,* growing 4 to 5 ft. high and producing quantities of bright yellow daisy-like flowers on long stems useful for cutting.

Tolerates a wide range of soils, including poor, dry soil, resists heat, and blooms in midsummer. Easily grown from seed sown outdoors from May to September and from root divisions in spring or fall.

Heuchera

Heuchera sanguinea (Coral Bells). Hardy perennial, growing 2 ft. high, forming a neat mound of heart-shaped leaves bearing long, slender flower spikes with dainty red, white or pink flowers. Blooming in May and June, heucheras are good for rock gardens, wild gardens and perennial borders, the long flower stems making them useful as a cut flower.

Prefers a sunny location, planted 16 in. apart, in a fertile, well-drained soil. Top dress with garden compost or well-decomposed animal manure each spring for best results. Lift, divide and replant clumps every third year in spring or fall.

Easily grown from seed, allowing 10 days for germination. Seed is tiny and can be started indoors or sown thinly outdoors in May for blooms the following spring.

Lavender

Lavendula vera. Hardy perennial, 2 ft. high, flowering

Lythrum

Lychnis (Maltese Cross)

June to September. Creates a dense, bushy plant with long, slender stems topped by clusters of tiny purple flowers which impart the famous lavender fragrance, especially when cut and dried in a cool, ventilated place.

Seed germination is slow, and plants will need mulching for protection in cold areas. Does well in a wide range of soils, especially good for rock gardens and herb gardens.

Liatris

Liatris pycnostachya (Blazing Star). Hardy perennial, 2 to 6 ft. high, used in borders and desirable as a cut flower. Long flower spikes resemble a bottle-brush and bloom in white or purple. Grows well in most garden soils, in sun or partial shade and is especially effective planted along stream banks or pond sides.

Blooms from midsummer to fall and is best propagated by root divisions made in early spring. It is also easily grown from seed started indoors in early March or sown directly outdoors after danger of frost. Space plants 20 in. apart. Seed germinates in 20 days.

Lunaria

Lunaria biennis (Honesty). Hardy biennial, 4 ft. high, grown principally for its silvery oval seed pods, which are useful alone as a dried flower arrangement or mixed with other everlasting flowers. The pink, mauve or white flowers appear in May or early June, the second season after sowing seed, followed by the decorative seed pods in fall. Dark colored outer membranes sometimes have to be peeled off to reveal the more desirable silvery inner membrane.

Easily grown from seeds sown directly into the garden from spring to midsummer and thinned to stand 2 ft. apart. Tolerates semishade and reseeds so readily it gives the impression of being a perennial.

Lupine

Lupinus polyphyllus. Hardy perennial, 3 ft. tall, used in borders and valued as a cut flower, although the flower spikes droop when cut. The flower spikes are packed with closely-set pea-shaped florets in red, white and blue, plus many bicolors. Especially effective when used in groups of 3 or 4 plants, spaced 12 in. apart, blooming in early summer when cool conditions favor flowering.

Lupines like their heads in the sun and their feet in the shade, preferring a moist well-drained soil in a sunny location. Easily grown from seed which is bullet-hard and needs soaking in water overnight before planting to ensure reliable germination. Sow outdoors in May or June, planting the seeds 1/4 in. deep and thinning plants to 10 in. apart. After blooming, cut off dead flower spikes to prevent weakening the plants. Although classed as perennials, lupines tend to exhaust themselves after several years and may need replenishing with new plants. A light mulch will help plants winter in northern areas. *Russell Hybrids* and *Minarette,* a dwarf strain, are considered to be the best named varieties.

Lychnis

Lychnis chalcedonica (Maltese Cross). Hardy perennial, 2 ft. high, growing clusters of bright scarlet flowers on long, slender stems from spring to midsummer. Does well in rock gardens and sunny borders, in a wide range of well-drained soils.

Propagate by seed sown outdoors in April or by root divisions made in fall.

Lythrum

Lythrum Salicaria (Purple Loosestrife). Hardy perennial, 6 ft. tall, blooming in July and August with masses of purple-pink flower spikes. Does best when planted in a moist, fertile soil in a sunny location, such as close to a pond or stream. Use sparingly in flower borders, since it can be overpowering, spreading 3 feet and more across.

Best grown from root divisions made in spring or fall and spaced 2 ft. apart. Plants from seed need starting in spring either indoors or out, allowing 15 days for germination.

| Monarda | Penstemon | Summer Phlox |

Monarda

Monarda didyma (Bee Balm, Bergamot). Hardy perennial, growing to 3 ft. high, flowering July and August, creating a dense cluster of ray-petalled, spidery flowers mostly in pink and red on long stems good for cutting. Thrives in most soils in sun or light shade. Use sparingly in the perennial border. One plant makes a striking display.

Divide and replant every third year in summer, spacing plants 8 in. apart, and mulching them the first year after the ground is frozen. Good near streams and at edge of woods. Easily grown from seeds in spring or summer, germinating in 15 days.

Penstemon

Penstemon murrayanus grandiflorus (Beardlip). Hardy perennial, growing to 3 ft. high, flowering May and June, with colorful flower spikes similar to snapdragons but with open mouths. Colors include white, pink, rose and crimson, lavender, and bicolors. Likes a sunny to partly shaded location and a fertile, well drained soil. Best used in a mass planting and good for cut flower arrangements.

Needs a sheltered location and mulching to survive severe winters. Space plants 12 in. apart in fall or early spring, or start from seeds in February or March, allowing 10 days for germination.

Phlox

Phlox decussata (Summer Phlox). Hardy perennial, growing to 3 ft., flowering July and August, with clusters of flowers in white, red, orange and purple. Likes a sunny position and a fertile, moist soil. Use in a mass planting or in clumps between shrubs. Space plants 18 in. apart in fall or spring, or start from seeds in October outside for germination the following spring. Seed sown indoors requires 30 days chilling in refrigerator to break dormancy, after which germination takes 25 days. Lifting and dividing roots every 3 years helps to ensure maximum bloom production. Otherwise, phlox are an extremely carefree display flower, valuable for cutting, and an indispensible feature of most perennial borders. To prevent mildew infestation, avoid watering plants from above so flowers and foliage keep dry. Cut off dead flower stems to prevent plants from going to seed, and mulch plants the first year after the ground freezes.

Phlox divaricata (Blue Phlox). Hardy perennial, 10 in. high, flowering in April and May with fragrant pale blue flowers. Tolerates some shade and is exquisite planted in a border with clumps of tulips and daffodils or in a rockery where it can create a dense carpet of bloom. Plant 8 in. apart in fall.

Phlox subulata (Creeping Phlox). Hardy perennial, 4 in. high, creating a dense flowering carpet of brilliant color in April. Colors include shades of white, red, blue and purple, lasting 2 weeks. Used extensively in rock gardens and dry slopes. Tolerates light shade, but enjoys full sun. Moss-like foliage stays green. Plant 8 in. apart in spring or fall, or start seeds indoors in fall or winter, chilling for 30 days in the refrigerator, after which seeds will germinate in 25 days. Divide and replant after flowering, every 3 years in confined spaces.

Platycodon

Platycodon grandiflorum (Balloon Flower). Hardy perennial, 20 in. high, flowering June until frost with lovely bell-shaped blue or white flowers resembling giant hare bells, ideal for borders. Needs full sun and a sandy or light loam soil with good drainage, and looks particularly decorative when planted in groups of several plants. Plant root divisions in spring or fall, spaced 12 in. apart, or start seeds indoors in February for blooms in summer, allowing 10 days for germination. Mulching to protect plants over winter is a wise precaution.

Poppy, Iceland

Papaver nudicaule. Hardy perennial, growing to 18 in. high, producing tufts of leaves and long-stemmed flowers with crepe-like petals in May and June, mostly in white, red, orange and yellow. Not suitable as a cut flower, however, since the flower stems collapse when cut.

Likes a sunny location in fertile garden soil with exceptional drainage. Plant outdoors in early spring or fall,

Salvia farinacea Blue Bedder   Rudbeckia   Platycodon   Oriental Poppy

spaced 2 ft. apart, or sow seeds directly into the garden in early spring. If started indoors, use peat pots, since they do not transplant well if the roots are disturbed. Germination generally takes 10 days. *Champagne Bubbles,* a vigorous hybrid mixture with larger, longer lasting flowers, is a recommended variety, flowering the first year from seed started indoors in January or February.

Poppy, Oriental

Papaver orientale. Hardy perennial, 2-1/2 ft. high, with the largest blooms and richest colors of any poppy, some measuring 6 in. across, and handsomely marked with black blotches at the base of each petal. Colors include white, pale pink, orange and blood red with some bicolors. Use in bold color groups on fertile, well-drained soil in a sunny but sheltered position, since they are susceptible to wind damage in exposed locations.

Space plants 12 in. apart in spring or fall, or sow seed directly into the garden from spring to midsummer. Since they do not transplant well, indoor sowings should be made into peat pots, ensuring no root disturbance on planting. Germination takes up to 20 days at 75 degree soil temperature. Recommended varieties: *Helen Elizabeth,* a cool pink, and *Bonfire,* a vivid fire-engine red.

Pyrethrum

Pyrethrum roseum (Painted Daisy). Hardy perennial,

growing to 30 in. high, flowering May, June and July with daisy-like flowers in white, shades of red, yellow and bicolors. Thrives in most soils that are well drained and exposed to the sun. Makes an eye-catching border perennial and valuable cut flower. Plant 15 in. apart in early spring, or start seeds March 1st indoors for June blooms in a soil temperature of 75 degrees for 21 days. Seeds sown outdoors from May to July will bloom the following year.

Rudbeckia

Rudbeckia hirta (Gloriosa Daisy, Black-eyed Susans). No other hardy perennial provides such a brilliant display of long lasting color as gloriosa daisies — or tetraploid rudbeckias. What's more, they can tolerate fierce summer heat and poor soil better than few other flowers, yet they are so hardy it's possible to get reliable germination from seed sown on top of snow. A better way to grow them, however, is to start seed indoors March 1st, and transplant well-established seedlings into the garden. This way they will perform like annuals, blooming the first year, then behaving like a perennial and coming up year after year, with even more blooms. Alternatively, seed sown outdoors 8 weeks before your last frost date will generally produce flowers the first season.

The huge daisy-like blooms are generally bright yellow, although there are bicolored varieties with mahogany markings. Also, there is a double

yellow form which is even more spectacular than the daisy-flowered kinds.

Growing 3 ft. high, gloriosa daisies produce their flowers on long stems that are excellent for cutting to make beautiful indoor flower arrangements, either by themselves or mixed in with zinnias and snapdragons.

In the perennial border as a display flower, they are magnificent, and planted in a massed bed, they are superb. Related to the wild rudbeckias (or black-eyed Susans) found growing along the waysides throughout America, these tetra-ploids are a relatively modern breeding achievement created by tripling the number of chromosomes through the use of a drug called colchicine. They are by far the most rewarding perennial grown in home gardens.

Salvia, Blue

Salvia farinacea. Hardy perennial growing to 3 ft. high, blooming from midsummer to frost with slender, graceful spires of deep blue flowers on long stems useful for cutting. Prefers a sunny or partly shaded location in the perennial border and a dry, well-drained soil.

Plant 18 in. apart in April or September from root divisions, or transplant seedlings after danger of frost from seed started indoors in March at 75 degree soil temperature. Seed germinates in 15 days. Recommended variety: *Blue Bedder,* a deep Wedgwood blue.

Stokesia

Siberian Wallflower

Sedum spectabile

Perennial Sweet Pea (Lathyrus)

Scabiosa

Scabiosa caucasica (Pincushion Flower). Hardy perennial, 3 ft. high, flowering all summer, and far superior to the annual type (*Scabiosa atropurpurea*). Exceptionally fine for cutting to make indoor flower arrangements, especially the misty blues, although white and lavender forms are available.

Sow seed outdoors in September, thinning to 18 in. apart for flowers the following June, or start indoors in peat pots March 1st at 80 degree soil temperature for 12 days to gain healthy transplants for July blooms. Propagate also by root division and cuttings. Needs a sunny location.

Sea Lavender

Limonium latifolia (Perennial Statice). Hardy perennial, 2 ft. high, flowering July to September with clusters of papery flowers resembling statice, in lavender-purple on twiggy stems. Colorful in the perennial border or rock garden, and valuable as an everlasting flower for dried arrangements.

Does well in average soil in a sunny location, especially seaside gardens. Plant 30 in. apart in

spring, using root divisions, or start seed outdoors during cool spring weather, allowing 15 days for germination.

Sedum

Sedum spectabile (Stonecrop). There are more than 300 species of sedum useful in the perennial border and rock garden, but for sheer beauty few can compare with *Sedum spectabile*, a hardy perennial growing 3 ft. high, flowering in late August with quantities of long, fleshy stems topped by flat, pale pink flower clusters which attract hoards of bees and butterflies.

Enjoys a dry soil in full sun, and is easily propagated from root divisions made in spring or fall spaced 12 in. apart.

Siberian Wallflower

Cheiranthus Allioni. Hardy perennial, 15 in. high, blooming in May and June with sprays of golden-orange flowers that resemble wallflowers. Good for massed beds and borders during cool weather. Does well in most soils in a sunny position. Useful in rock gardens and as a cut flower. Space plants 12 in. apart, sowing seed outdoors in June where the plants are to bloom, for

flowers the following season. Sown indoors in February at 70 degree temperature for 10 days, they will flower in late summer. Much more dependable than their cousins the *English Wallflower*, which does well only in coastal areas of California and the Pacific Northwest.

Stokesia

Stokesia cyanea. Hardy perennial 15 in. high, flowering from July to August with masses of blue flowers resembling giant cornflowers on plants with a spreading, bush habit. Excellent as a massed bed display or as clumps in the rock garden.

Needs a sunny location and a light soil, planted 18 in. apart in May from root divisions. Seed sown directly into the garden in July will provide plants that bloom the following summer if given winter protection of a mulch in northern areas. Seed sown indoors in February will produce plants for fall flowering. Germination takes up to 20 days.

Sweet Pea, Perennial

Lathyrus latifolia. Hardy perennial, covering the ground with dense vines spreading 5 to 6 ft. Can be trained up a trellis.

Johnny Jump Up

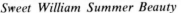

Sweet William Summer Beauty   *Tritoma (Red Hot Poker)*

Flowers July to September with white, rose and pink flowers resembling annual sweet peas, but smaller.

Succeeds in most soils, and tolerates drought, creating an excellent ground cover for dry slopes and requiring little or no care. Also excellent for erosion control. Sow seed indoors in March or outdoors in May, spacing plants 2 ft. apart. Also propagate by root divisions. Seed germinates in 20 days.

Sweet William
Dianthus barbatus. Hardy biennial, available in dwarf and tall varieties up to 18 in. high, flowering from April to June with clusters of bright bicolored florets. Some annual forms are available, such as *Wee Willie* and *Summer Beauty.* Gives a good display in most soils in a sunny position, and self seeds readily.

Biennial Sweet Williams can be sown outdoors from April 15th to August 15th for blooms the following spring on plants spaced 12 in. apart. Annual Sweet Williams can be sown indoors February 15th for July flowering or outdoors in May for September flowers. Seed germinates in 5 days.

Tritoma
Kniphofia Uvaria (Red Hot Poker). Also known as Kniphofia. Hardy perennial, 4 ft. tall, flowering June to September with best flower displays in cool weather. Plants grow in thick clumps with tropical-looking sword-shaped leaves, producing long flower stems topped by white, red, orange, yellow and bicolored "pokers", created by scores of tubular florets.

Good as highlights in the perennial border and for dramatic cut-flower arrangements. Needs a sunny location, and thrives even in poor, dry soil, tolerating drought. Propagate from root cuttings set 18 in. apart and from seeds started indoors in April at 80 degree soil temperature or outdoors in June. Germination takes up to 20 days. In northern areas mulch with 6 in. of straw to protect from severe winters.

Veronica
Veronica spicata (Speedwell). Hardy annual, growing 18 in. high, flowering June and July with tall spikes of blue, pink and white flowers, excellent for rock gardens. A dense colony of plants in a sunny perennial border is

effective, and it is useful as a cut flower. Divide and replant roots in spring or fall, planting 18 in. apart, or sow seed outdoors in blooming positions about May 15, germinating in 15 days. Recommended varieties: *Saraband*, a light blue, and *Crater Lakes*, a deep blue. Taller species, such as *Veronica exultata*, grow to 5 ft.

Viola
Viola cornuta (Tufted Pansies). Hardy perennial, 6 in. high, blooming July and August with flowers resembling miniature pansies in shades of red, white, blue and yellow. Fine in rock gardens, container plantings and as an edging to beds or borders. Does best in a cool, fertile soil, slightly shaded. Blooms first year from seed if sown indoors in February, germinating at 70 degrees for 10 days. Space plants 6 in. apart when set into permanent positions. Although truly perennials, they are best treated as annuals, starting from seed or providing new plants each year since hot summers tend to weaken them too much for successful overwintering. Popular *Johnny Jump-Ups* belong to this class and self-seed spectacularly.

47

Bearded Iris and Relatives

Japanese Iris

One of the most satisfying perennials you can grow in your garden is bearded iris. Easy to grow, the shiny green sword-like leaves are decorative for most of the year, the plants multiply rapidly, and the color range is so extensive you could never hope to collect every known variety.

Although bearded iris thrive in a wide range of soils, they respond better to a soil rich in humus, well drained and fed with a fertilizer low in nitrogen and high in phosphorus. An application of bone meal (high in phosphorous) every spring and fall will produce the best flowers.

As iris clumps spread and multiply, you should break up the clumps with a garden fork and replant, adding fresh soil and fertilizer. Iris swapping is a popular springtime activity. What you admire in your neighbor's garden can be yours in return for a few root divisions of the colors he admires among your collection. They can be lifted and replanted at any time of year — even in full bloom.

When planting a new bed or border, choose a sunny location. At least half a day of sunshine is necessary for good flowers. Plant the fleshy rhizomes 1 inch deep and 2 feet apart; divide again every 3 to 4 years.

Colors in iris range from white through yellow, red and blue to almost black. Many produce combinations of colors and some are exotically freckled.

Blue Sapphire is one of the finest light blues, with graceful arching petals and a heavy golden-yellow beard that contrasts beautifully with the cool petal colors. *Roccoco* is a magnificent two-tone pure white, richly edged with bright blue. The beard is deep yellow and the flowers reach enormous size. *Black Swan* will satisfy those looking for the ultimate in dark iris. The almost black petals are velvety smooth and very wide. *Cloud cap* is probably the largest flowered pink. Another feature is its bright tangerine beard.

The colors and combinations go on and on, and each year the hybridizers produce more and more exotic color combinations. Discover your own favorite colors. Admire them in the garden and marvel at their long lasting qualities indoors as a cut flower, imparting a hint of spicy fragrance.

Bulbous Dutch iris and Japanese iris are also worth space in your garden. Bronze, white, yellow and blue are the main Dutch iris colors. They require planting in fall in a sunny, well-drained location, and look their best planted in clumps between shrubs in a sunny border.

Japanese iris prefer a rich, moist acid soil, and few plants can rival their beauty when planted at the margins of a pond, lake or stream. Plant crowns 2 inches deep and 18 inches apart in early fall or spring. White, pink, blue and purple are the principal colors, plus some exotic bicolors.

Left *This healthy clump of bearded iris, Desert Song, increases each year with the help of bone meal applied in spring and fall.*

Bearded iris, Mount Trimp, *displays perfect form — graceful upward arching standard petals, heavily veined wide fall petals, and a bright conspicuous "beard."*

Bearded iris, Color Carnival (*left*) *and* Desert Song. *No other hardy perennial can match the color range of bearded iris, and a border of assorted colors in late spring can be breathtaking.*

White Japanese iris planted among stone outcrops near a stream with smooth stone pebbles for mulch and decorative appeal

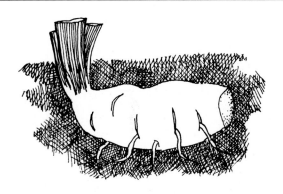

Diagram above shows proper planting depth for bearded iris.

Diagram below shows how a clump of bearded iris can be divided.

Bearded iris, Rich Reward, *grows huge, spectacular golden-yellow flowers and deep yellow beard.*

Bearded iris, Dancer's Veil, *is a beautiful blue and white bicolor of perfect form.*

Hardy bulbous Dutch iris, Wedgwood, *interplanted with tender ranunculus — an effect possible in areas with mild climates.*

Glorious Garden Lilies—
Queen of the Perennials

Japanese Auratum Lilies

The true family of lilies is one of the most confusing in all the flower world. Among many imposters are lily of the valley, calla lilies, day lilies, plantain lilies and spider lilies. Lilium, the true lilies, are the most showy of all, and skilled hybridizers, such as Jan de Graaff of Oregon, have created some sensational varieties.

Many of these new hybrids are so exotic in their beauty it's difficult to believe they are hardy and easy-to-grow over most of the United States — but they are. There's a place in everyone's garden for lilies. They look beautiful just about anywhere — in massed beds, singly between shrubs, in groups along a perennial border, in the sun or in light shade.

It's unfortunate that lilies have been associated so much with funerals. The staid, virgin white madonna lily certainly is grown extensively for funerals and at Easter. But there are other groups of lilies that bear little resemblance to the madonna and will liven up your flower garden, some of them with flowers the size of dinner plates, striped and freckled in vibrant colors.

Most regal of all are the Oriental Hybrids with enchanting names and huge spectacular flowers up to 10 inches across. *Empress of India* stands 5 feet tall, blooms in August, and displays 8 to 10 enormous flowers the color of ripe watermelons. *Imperial Silver* is a pure transluscent white, heavily spotted with a tinge of yellow at the petal centers. These magnificent specimen flowers bloom on 6-foot-tall plants, and just one or two will highlight your garden. *Imperial Gold* and *Imperial Crimson* are other colors in this gorgeous strain of lilies.

Jamboree, another outstanding Oriental Hybrid, has such delicate form and intense coloring you would imagine it to be highly temperamental and require the skill of a professional gardener to grow it. Happily, the opposite is true. *Jamboree* is a hardy, disease resistant aristocrat, full of hybrid vigor, easy to grow and pleasantly fragrant. The deep crimson flowers are heavily spotted, and its lovely arching petals sweep back to display the full color effect. On full grown plants there are often 14 flowers and up to 30 secondary buds.

Thunderbolt is a deep orange Oriental Hybrid with 20 or more large flowers crowding each stem, making it an unusually fine display flower for the garden, reaching to a height of 6 feet.

The Aurelian hybrids are another distinctive class, mainly July-blooming, and predominating in trumpet-shaped flowers. *Black Dragon* is a superlative strain. The inside of the flower is pure white, while the outside is dark brown, margined white. Its vigor is remarkable, producing plants that will stand 6 feet tall in only average soil. It bears a dozen or more trumpet flowers 6 inches across, slightly scented, in a perfect candelabra effect. *Golden Splendor* is similar to *Black Dragon,* but is a rich buttercup yellow that shimmers in the sunlight.

The Asiatic hybrids make superb cut flowers, and most of them are exquisite when planted in a massed bed. They include tiger lily hybrids with charming pendant flowers and chalice-shaped flowers growing upright. *Enchantment* is an upright form well suited for pot culture. June-flowering, its nasturtium red color blazes in the sun, 16 and more flowers to a stem. *Croesus* is a golden-yellow version of *Enchantment* and the two combine beautifully in a mixed bed. Among the Turk's cap lilies, *Amber Gold* has outstanding beauty. The rich yellow petals have deep maroon spots, and the 3-inch-diameter flowers have prominent stamens with brown-red pollen.

The time to plant lily bulbs is spring or fall. Plant in a well-drained location to a depth about 3 times the depth of the bulb. Nearly all lilies thrive in full sun or partial shade. They are gross feeders and root deeply, needing a soil that is rich in humus and well-balanced plant foods. A good mulch of well-decomposed manure, rich compost or decayed leaf mold should be applied several times during the growing season to bring out the best in them.

Remove old flowers as they become unattractive and try to prevent seed pods from developing. This will allow the plant to achieve maximum bulb development and assure next year's flower crop. Lily flowers make beautiful indoor flower arrangements, but take care not to cut too much stem length or foliage since these are needed to build for next year's growth. If mice or shrews are a menace in your garden, plant rodent repellent flakes with the bulbs or surround your plantings with fine wire mesh.

Lilies are lovely in pots. The potting soil should be 2 parts sandy loam, 1 part leaf mold and 1 part sand. An inch of gravel in the bottom of the pot will help to provide adequate drainage.

Turk's cap lilies combine with rhododendron and ferns to create a beautiful corner planting in semishade.

Among the largest-flowered of all garden lilies is Imperial Crimson, *here growing in a shade garden.*

Easiest to grow of all lilies is the sweet-scented Regal, growing blooms up to 5 inches across in July.

Peonies—
The Lovely and the Magnificent

Herbaceous Peony

Two kinds of hardy peonies have won the hearts of America — the familiar herbaceous peony in double and single forms from Europe, and the much more majestic tree peonies, revered in the Imperial gardens of China and Japan and so breathtakingly beautiful it is difficult to believe they are hardy. Tree peonies bloom in May and June, several weeks ahead of the earliest herbaceous peonies.

Herbaceous peonies are the most widely cultivated because they are easiest to grow. Variety names generally are American or European, such as *Bowl of Cream, Big Ben* and *Raspberry Sundae*, while variety names of the more sophisticated tree peonies flaunt exquisite Oriental names, such as *Tama Fuyo,* meaning "jewelled lotus," *Momoyama,* meaning "mountain of peach blossoms" and *Hana Den,* meaning "palace of flowers."

Tree Peonies

One well-grown Japanese tree peony will outshine an entire border of herbaceous peonies, but they are more expensive and require a little more care to get them established. Individual blooms measure up to 10 inches across and are fragrantly scented, with as many as 50 or more blooms open at one time and 100 or more total buds and blooms.

The term *tree peony* (or *Moutan* as the Chinese call it) is misleading since the plants grow more like a bushy shrub 3 to 4 feet high, by 3 feet across, the decorative foliage staying lush and green until fall, when it changes to autumn hues, then dies down. It is extremely hardy, but in some warm areas it makes new growth a little too

early and the young shoots become vulnerable to cold winds or heavy frosts.

The real secret of success is to choose a spot that is sheltered and does not get early morning sun, such as a shrub or perennial border on the west side of a stone wall or hedge.

Unlike the herbaceous peonies, tree peony roots should be set comparatively deep — up to 6 inches — in planting holes that have been deeply dug — at least 1-1/2 feet — and well fertilized with garden compost — but not animal manure — to encourage healthy root development. Around the outside of the hole and in the bottom, spread 2 handfuls of a commercial fertilizer low in nitrogen, but high in phosphorus and potash. They are gross feeders and will benefit from subsequent applications of garden compost and bone meal after flowers have ceased to bloom. April and October are ideal planting times.

A valuable attribute of the tree peony is shade tolerance, plus a more extensive color range than herbaceous peonies, including yellow.

As long ago as the 17th century, traders and French missionaires to China told of the wild tree peonies growing in the Moutan Mountains in such profusion they filled the air with a heady fragrance. Today's garden hybrids are the result of centuries of selection and breeding by Japanese and Chinese breeders.

A special group of tree peonies are called the Lutea hybrids, the best of which were created by an American hybridizer, Professor A.P. Saunders. They excel in fragrant yellow hues.

Some outstanding tree peony varieties to consider are *Harvest*, a semi-double yellow Lutea hybrid with a

Dividing Peonies

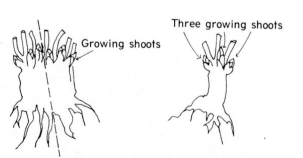

Planting Grafted Tree Peony

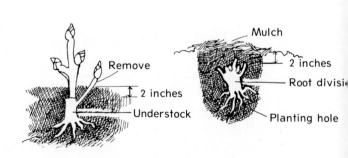

rich orange center surrounding a whorl of golden stamens; *Suffruticosa*, with pure white purple based petals; *Hakuo-Jishi*, a fully double pure white Japanese hybrid with a nest of gigantic golden-yellow stamens; and *Tama Fuyo*, a large early blooming double pink.

Herbaceous Peonies

Blooming in late May and June, herbaceous peonies like the sun and thrive in a deep fertile soil, helping to fill the void between the colorful spring-flowering bulbs and summer annuals. Since plants need 3 feet of space, they should be used sparingly in the perennial border or to create a "hedge" effect, planted side-by-side in alternating color groups.

Dig generous planting holes at least 1-1/2 feet deep and fill with good garden soil enriched with organic matter, such as well-decomposed manure or garden compost. The soil should never be allowed to dry out, and mulching is advisable in exposed positions. Fall and spring are both suitable planting times although fall is preferred.

Plant roots of herbaceous peonies no more than 2 inches below ground level. They are propagated by root division, and any piece of root with an "eye" is capable of growing a new plant, although 3 to 5 eye divisions is preferable.

Outstanding varieties include *Edulis Superba*, a fragrant double pink, *Kelway's Glorious*, a large sweetly scented double white, *Raspberry Sundae*, a massive double white with raspberry petals clustered in the center, and *Jaycee*, a patented large double red with petals tipped silver.

Above   *Herbaceous peony* Edulis Superba.

Below   *Single-flowered pink hybrid tree peony,* Bowl of Beauty.

Peony garden at Winterthur, Delaware. Variety shown is Janice *a semi-double early herbaceous hybrid peony.*

Her Majesty—
The Rose

Yellow Grandiflora Rose

Roses are such an important part of flower gardens throughout the world that an entire industry has been created around them — an industry which supports a number of specialist rose breeders, specialist rose growers, and even a specialist mail-order industry.

Kinds of Roses

The most popular kinds of roses for home gardens fit into four major categories, although the official classifications for roses carry many others.

Hybrid Tea. These are the most popular modern roses for flower beds and display gardens, since they are hardy and generally grow the largest flowers. The classic "urn" shaped blooms are a common feature of this class. They are the best for cutting, since each flower grows on a single stem. Heaviest bloom occurs in June and September. Plants grow from 3 to 6 feet, depending on climate. The famous roses, *Peace* (yellow tinged pink) and *Chrysler Imperial* (crimson), fit into this group.

Floribunda. Although smaller-flowered than hybrid teas, floribundas give a greater density of bloom over a longer period. They are generally hardier, lower growing and bushier than the hybrid teas, forming their flowers in clusters or "sprays". They are most effective where an impressive mass of color is desired, growing just 3 to 4 feet in most areas. Many outstanding single-flowered types belong to this class, resembling wild roses in a vivid color range. *Circus* (bicolored orange and pink) and *Fashion* (rosy-red) are outstanding examples of this class.

Climbers. In great demand to create rose arbors and hedges, climbers are capable of reaching heights up to 20 feet. Trained along a fence or up a trellis, they produce incredible quantities of bloom, especially in June, of which *Blaze* (scarlet-red) is the best example. Best of the hedging roses are *The Fairy* (whitish-pink) and *Robin-Hood* (rosy-red), creating such a dense growth that they require no support and can be left undisturbed without pruning.

Miniatures. Outdoors, miniatures are good for edging rose beds, rock gardens and containers. Indoors they will make a delightful pot plant when given sufficient light. Growing barely 12 inches tall, each plant almost smothers itself in tiny thimble-size blooms — perfect in form and far less demanding than any of the other rose classes.

Rose Hedge, Robin Hood

How to Grow Roses

Roses have deservedly developed a reputation for being easy to grow and reliable in a wide range of soil conditions and climates, and it's easy to understand why there is such a strong following of rose enthusiasts throughout the world. Books have been written on the subject of roses alone, but boiling everything down to essentials there are only five areas that demand special mention. They are **planting, feeding, pruning, pests and diseases** and **winter care.**

Planting. Although spring and fall are appropriate times for planting roses, by far the best times are October and November. Dig planting holes 1-1/2 feet deep and wide enough for the roots to be spread out, mixing peat moss, leaf mold or good garden compost into the bottom soil, adding a flower fertilizer high in phosphorous for good root development.

Before planting, cut away dead or damaged roots and stand the roots in water for several hours to counter any effect of dehydration during shipment to the store or through the mails. Planting depth is indicated by the previous soil mark on the stem. Plants should be spaced 18 inches apart.

As you fill the planting hole, add water and tread soil firmly in place around the roots. Mulch the surface with any kind of organic material, such as grass clippings, shredded leaves or straw.

Feeding. Many packaged rose fertilizers are readily available for applying around rose roots in spring or fall, and roses respond well to foliar feeding of general foliar fertilizers sprayed on to the leaves. Mulching each fall with well-decomposed animal manure or garden compost is also beneficial.

Pruning. Except for climbing roses and hedging roses, vigorous pruning is essential to keep roses within bounds and maintain healthy free-flowering plants. March is a good month to do this — just before new leaf growth begins. Using sharp pruning tools, first cut out any dead or weak branches, making each cut at an angle just above a bud point.

Bush roses need pruning especially hard, to within 4 or 5 buds from the soil line, or 1-1/2 feet.

Pruning a Rose

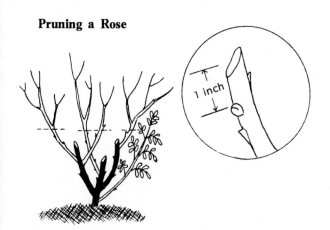

Planting a Rose

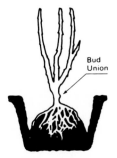

Bud Union

1. Place bush on dirt mound. Add or remove dirt to raise bud union to proper level.

2. Add dirt to fill ¾ of hole, working firmly around roots to eliminate air pockets.

3. Fill remaining depression with water to ground level and let it soak into soil.

4. Tramp down; fill with dirt; leave it loose. Mound soil or mulch around base.

An old-fashioned rose garden features white picket fence, rustic arbor and beds mulched with coco bean hulls.

Pests and Diseases. Unfortunately, roses are susceptible to more pests and diseases than any other flower in the garden, although some varieties are more susceptible to attack than others. But there are many effective controls which can be used against them.

The chief insect pests are chewing and sucking insects, such as Japanese beetles, aphids and thrips, which can be controlled organically or chemically by regular spraying or dusting.

Powdery mildew (a white discoloration on the leaves) is the most common fungus disease, and there are packaged rose fungicides to control it. Regular inspection of rose plants in spring and summer will ensure early detection and cure.

Winter care. If you live in an area in which temperatures fall to 10 degrees above zero or less, you might want to consider some of these precautions.

Do not feed the roses past September 1st. Feeding roses too late in the season can artificially induce a growth period at a time when the plant should be going dormant.

When cutting your roses back in the fall, leave some latitude for freezing — don't prune lower than 1-1/2 feet above the ground; at this height, several inches of cane can freeze and there will still be a live portion. Do your final pruning in the spring just before the plants break dormancy.

In regions that definitely require protection, mounding is a common method. Bring in soil from another area rather than scraping it up from the bed. Mound the soil in and around the bush to a height of 12 inches or more. Do not use materials such as leaves that will mat or that are too dense to permit air circulation to the roots.

Polyanthus rose, The Fairy, *tumbles down a dry rock wall, adding color to an outdoor picnic area and a touch of wild beauty to the naturalistic setting, featuring a high waterfall in the background.*

Rose garden at Lyndhurst Castle, New York, displays a romantic all-white theme, with arbors of climbing roses and a gazebo as a focal point.

56

Zambra

My Top Ten
Rose Selection

Lady Elgin

Peace

Fashion

The Fairy

Chicago Peace

Chrysler Imperial

Circus

Miss All America Beauty

Tiffany

Spring-Flowering Bulbs for Fall Planting

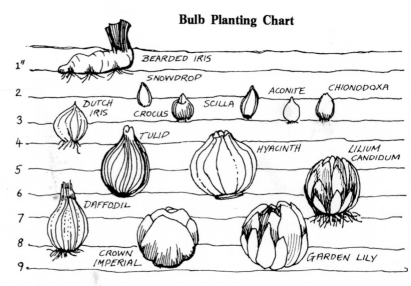

Double Tulips

If you've always promised yourself a beautiful spring garden full of colorful spring bulbs, fall is the time to start planting. And it's easy. With flowering bulbs, just pop them in the dirt and cover them up. It's as simple as that — almost!

Actually, there are a few basic questions people keep asking about bulbs. Know the answers and you'll have the most glorious displays of flowers in early spring, year after year. Here they are:

When to Plant

Anytime after Labor Day. Vacations are over, the kids are back to school, and you'll have plenty of time to plant hundreds of bulbs. However, if you get delayed you can still plant your bulbs up to the beginning of December in most northern states. The ground hasn't usually frozen up by then. The tulips will take it without any side effects, and the only difference it will make to daffodils is delay their blooming in the spring by a week or two.

What Type of Soil

Just about any type of soil with good drainage will produce acceptable results for most bulbs, but for really spectacular, exhibition-size blooms the most important ingredients are humus and bone meal. If your soil lacks humus, it can be provided from composted leaves, grass clippings and kitchen wastes. When it's well decomposed, just dig it into your bulb beds prior to planting. A quicker way of providing humus is to mix in peat moss, available in bales from garden centers.

Bone meal is a source of phosphorus, highly beneficial to flowering bulbs. Add it to beds and naturalized plantings twice a year — in spring and fall. If you have vast areas of naturalized bulbs, such as daffodils, superphosphate is an economical substitute.

How to Plant

Naturally, each bulb variety has a different planting depth and space requirement, and these are given on the package when you buy bulbs. Daffodils and Crown Imperials tolerate shade magnificently, and they will keep coming up every year. Tulips prefer plenty of sun. The Darwin, May-flowering and cottage tulips are best replanted every year, but the early-flowering species can stay put year after year. Mice and other rodents relish tulips, hyacinths and crocus bulbs, but daffodils are poisonous to them. If your garden is plagued by these pests, stay with the daffodils or plant rodent repellent flakes with the bulbs.

For best effect group separate colors together. A few bulbs of all one color usually make a much better display than a mixture. Bold contrasts are also effective — such as red and white or purple and yellow tulips. Always choose top-size bulbs — the bigger the bulb the better the bloom.

Hundreds of daffodils naturalized at Fordhook Farms, near Doylestown, Pennsylvania

Bulb Planting Chart

What to Plant

This is always a matter of personal preference, but bulb breeders have produced some magnificent new varieties which deserve special attention.

When choosing bulbs, it's good to remember that they bloom in three distinct seasons — early, midseason and late. By selecting varieties from each season, a garden can stay colorful from early April until late May, something new coming along all the time.

Daffodils. As a garden investment, nothing equals the dependable, carefree daffodil — a plant that truly thrives on neglect. It's so foolproof that even bulb-hungry mice and shrews won't bother it. Daffodils thrive in any well-cultivated, well-drained garden soil. Most are suitable for naturalizing — especially at the edge of trees, streams and on sunny banks. A classic setting is beneath a clump of silver birch.

Daffodils multiply so rapidly they may crowd each other out after only a few years, causing them to produce more leaves than flowers. When this occurs, dig them up in midsummer, separate and replant 5 inches apart. When choosing daffodils for your own garden, don't overlook the "old-timers." They're generally less expensive and very dependable. *King Alfred* (all yellow), *Beersheba* (pure white) and *Music Hall* (white petals, golden trumpet) belong to this group.

Newer daffodils that are unusual and worth the extra cost are *Roulette* (a large white with wide crinkled crown flushed with coral), *Salome* (a sensational new pink trumpet daffodil with gleaming white petals), and *Stadium* (pure white petals and an enormous wide yellow crown).

Tulips. These popular flowers have come a long way from the time they were discovered more than 400 years ago in the gardens of Constantinople by a Flemish diplomat who brought them to Europe. Holland took an early interest in them and built a flourishing industry of breeding, growing and exporting to all corners of the world.

Alexander Dumas' classic adventure story, "The Black Tulip," was a figment of his imagination at the time of writing. But now black tulips are common.

Today Holland still leads the world in raising tulips, and the many tulips now available fill a wide range of needs. Tulips not only look like tulips. Some look like water lilies. Others look like peonies. And there are numerous other variations in between.

The biggest tulip breeding breakthrough of recent years has been the creation of a whole new race of tulips called the Darwin Hybrids. These aristocrats are the offspring of a cross between the old *Darwin* tulips and the brilliantly colored early-blooming *Fosteriana* tulips. As the color range increases each year, these new Darwin Hybrids seem certain to overtake all other types in popularity.

Best of the bunch are the bizarre *Gudoshnik, Jewel of Spring* (a fantastically large sulphur-yellow with black center), and *Elizabeth Arden* (a delicate rose-pink).

Tulip Rosy Wings, *the finest of all cottage tulips backlighted against a clear spring sky.*

Daffodil Scarlet O'Hara, *an outstanding deep yellow with a deep orange, frilled trumpet.*

Tulips Jewel of Spring *grouped between evergreen shrubs present a glorious sight.*

Kaufmanniana water lily tulips are the earliest to bloom, and increase in loveliness year after year with adequate feedings of bone meal.

Hyacinths. The easiest flowering bulbs to grow indoors in pots or bowls are hyacinths, filling the air with a wonderful fragrance. A favorite way to grow them is in special hyacinth bowls filled only with water, since the bulb itself has enough energy to bloom without soil or nutrients. However, unless bulbs have been pre-conditioned to flower successfully indoors, they should first spend at least 8 weeks in a cold, dark place, such as an unheated garage or darkened cold frame, in order to ensure vigorous root development before they are brought indoors to flower in a sunny window.

Although colors include white, blue, red and pale yellow, in my experience the pale pinks give the best outdoor display, planted in groups of a dozen or more bulbs.

Crocus. These bulbs can be naturalized on sunny slopes and lawns, although care should be taken not to mow the lawn where they grow until the leaves have died down in June. Best effects are achieved by planting crocus in color groups — all white, all yellow, all blue or all striped in clumps of a dozen or more. Crocus also make a stunning border, especially when the separate colors are alternated in groups.

Crocus are widely grown indoors, especially in strawberry planters, but like all other flowering bulbs for indoor display, they need a cold dark spell of 8 to 10 weeks before they are brought into the sunlight to flower indoors.

A whole host of other small flowering bulbs are also worth growing for early spring color, including Siberian Squill, Grape Hyacinth, Bluebells (*Scilla campanulata*), Winter Aconite and Snowdrops.

A massed bed of all pink hyacinths, such as variety Lady Elgin, *will fill the air with a haunting fragrance.*

Pickwick, the striped crocus, naturalized on a sunny lawn

Shimmering yellow winter aconite is earliest of all bulbs to bloom, even before snowdrops.

Clumps of snowdrops do well under trees and left to naturalize.

This giant allium can grow as tall as a person.

Giant Allium Grows Tall as a Man

Allium. A magnificent flower guaranteed to produce gasps of surprise from passers-by is the Giant Allium (*Allium giganteum*), standing tall as a man in your own garden. A true member of the onion family — but lacking any odor — its gigantic bulb sends up a slender green shoot in the spring to a height of 5 feet and more, producing huge 10-inch diameter purple blooms in June. Ball-shaped and visible from a great distance, the flowers stay open for fully 2 weeks. Growing up — rather than out — there's room in every garden for this towering giant.

Planted in fall right up till the ground freezes, the bulbs will thrive anywhere in fertile soil that has good drainage. They need a good planting depth — about 18 inches in full sun. Once established, they live for years and will multiply almost as freely as daffodils, providing generous applications of bone meal are given in spring and fall.

Other ornamental onions which belong to the flower garden rather than the vegetable plot are smaller flowered but equally easy to grow, and ideal for naturalizing. The Red Allium (*Allium ostrowskianum*) is dwarf, only six inches tall, and good for rock gardens. Star of Persia (*Allium albophilosum*) has larger umbels covered with star-shaped violet flowers easily dried for flower arrangements. Yellow Allium (*Allium Moly*) produces myriads of bright yellow flowers on tropical-like plants. They contrast beautifully with spreading juniper and other low-growing conifers.

All the ornamental onions — large and small — deserve to be more widely grown in perennial gardens.

How to Force Bulbs for Winter Blooms Indoors

Forcing bulbs to bloom indoors during bleak winter months is great fun and a rewarding challenge.

Before bulbs will flower — either indoors or out — they need a prolonged cold spell to develop an adequate root system, then a gradual warming period to produce flowers. Winter and spring provide these conditions naturally, and the object of bulb forcing is to imitate these conditions over a shorter period so blooms appear much earlier than normal.

As a general rule, daffodils and tulips require at least 12 weeks of "cold." The cold treatment is best provided by placing the potted-up bulbs outdoors in a rooting bed or indoors in a cold, dark area. The temperature in the rooting location should be 40 to 50 degrees. Any temperature below this range will lengthen the rooting period. Above 50 degrees, it may prevent rooting altogether. A cold, dark basement, unheated garage or a shed are favorite locations.

The traditional outdoor rooting bed is made by digging a pit in a sheltered position 1 inch deeper than the height of your tallest bulb container. Set the pots close together and cover with 6 inches of light soil. Water thoroughly, and as cold weather sets in, cover with a protective mulch of straw or leaves to keep the pit at an even temperature.

After 12 weeks of cooling, check one or two of the pots to see if the roots are visible through the drainage hole and the shoots are about 2 inches high. If roots are not visible, turn the pot upside down and tap the sides gently to remove the contents and see if the root system is well developed. If the roots are not substantially long or showing through the drainage hole, return the container for another 2 weeks of cold treatment.

Once rooting has been completed, the containers should be moved to a semi dark area for a week or two at about 60 degrees. After this period of acclimation, the pots can be placed in a living room with normal light at house temperatures not exceeding 72 degrees.

Containers for forcing should be at least twice as high as the bulbs to allow for sufficient root growth. A good planting mixture is one part garden soil, one part peat moss and one part sand. Broken crocks or stones in the bottom will prevent the drainage hole from clogging. Press bulbs into the soil so they almost touch each other. Cover within a half inch of the top. Tips of the bulbs should protrude above the soil surface. Label each container noting the date planted, the variety and color. Water regularly and your fall planted bulbs will fill your home with fragrance and color.

Bulb Planting in Warm Climates

Flowering bulbs *can* be planted in frost-free areas of the United States by storing the bulbs in the bottom of a refrigerator at 40-50 degrees for 12 weeks until January 1, then planting outside to grow and flower.

Beauty from Bulbs

A bed of mixed daffodils at Peddler's Village, Lahaska, Pennsylvania, proves that the less expensive bulb mixtures can give as good a display as separate colors.

The largest flowered tulip of all, Pinkeen, *is also one of the earliest to flower in spring.*

Daffodil Moon Orbit *displays lemon-yellow petals and pale trumpet.*

Early double-tulip, Fringed Beauty, *has bizarre coloring and form.*

Pristine White Emperor *tulips, the earliest pure white, is planted here in front of an espaliered Atlas cedar.*

Beautiful bed of Darwin hybrid tulips, largest and most spectacular of early flowering tulips

Crown Imperials— The Royal Flower

An unusual spring-flowering bulb to plant in fall is the Crown Imperial (*Fritillaria imperialis*). Although quite a recent introduction into American gardens, Europeans have cherished it for centuries as a handsome, tall-growing border plant that loves to be planted in clumps between shrubs at the edge of a lawn or close to the house.

It is called Crown Imperial because after its discovery in the gardens of Turkey, it became the favorite flower of Maximillian II, Emperor of Austria, who grew it extensively in his Imperial Gardens in Vienna as far back as 1576.

When the bulbs sprout in early spring, the stems and foliage are not unlike lilies, but crowned with a circle of pendant-like bell-shaped blooms surmounted by a majestic green plume of slender leaves. The flowers are mainly orange-red and yellow, opening out in early April.

Since the bulbs have a hollow center, they should be planted on their sides to prevent water settling in the center and rotting out the bulb. Plant 8 inches deep in clusters of all one color, 12 inches apart. Once established they can be left undisturbed for years, especially when twice-yearly applications of bone meal or a high phosphorous fertilizer are made in early spring and fall to keep them healthy.

Oriental Splendor, *a Greigii tulip, and yellow Crown Imperials combine to make a magnificent border display.*

Summer-Flowering Bulbs for Spring Planting

Dwarf Cannas

To most homeowners, bulb-flowering time is spring, and planting time is fall. That's how it is with tulips and daffodils, plus many other related flowering plants. However, there is another large group of spectacular, easy-to-grow flowering bulbs which bloom in summer from spring planting. Some are not really bulbs, but fleshy roots and tubers that are treated like bulbs. Following is a listing of the most spectacular kinds for garden display.

Amaryllis, Hardy

Lycoris squamigera (Magic lily). Lavender-pink, trumpet-shaped flowers are clustered together in sets of 8 to 12 blooms on 3 ft. stalks. The leaves appear in spring, die down in July, and magically are followed by the magnificent flower stalks.

Makes an exquisite cut flower and succeeds in any well-drained soil. Best effect is achieved by planting the bulbs in clusters spaced 10 in. apart to a depth of 5 in. Hardy even in northern states, the bulbs can be left in the ground over winter and will multiply freely if nourished each spring and fall with dressings of bone meal or a phosphorous-rich fertilizer.

Canna

Canna hortensis. Commonly called Indian Shot because its bullet-hard seeds were once used as gun shot in the West Indies. The richly colored torch-like flower heads bloom all summer in shades of red, pink, yellow (some speckled) on 4 ft. stems. An added bonus is the tropical-looking green and bronze foliage.

Dwarf varieties are also available, but it is the tall kinds which are more popular as a lawn center-piece or a bold border.

Roots with 2 or 3 eye divisions should be planted after all danger of frost, 2 in. deep and 18 in. apart. They need a sunny location and a rich moist soil for best display. For earliest blooms plants can be started indoors in pots, hardened off in a cold frame, and transplanted to the garden after all danger of frost.

In northern states when the leaves die down in fall, the tender roots can be lifted, dried and stored in vermiculite or peat moss at 50 degree temperatures. In milder climates, such as the Pacific coast and southern states, they can be left in the ground.

Dahlia, Exhibition

In addition to a select group of dwarf dahlias easily grown from seed, there is a large group of exhibition dahlias popularly grown from tubers — some reaching 4 ft. in height with individual blooms up to 10 in. across.

They like a light, well-drained, fertile soil, in full sun, but not too exposed since the fleshy stems break easily. Watering during dry spells is essential since they are thirsty plants.

Plant tubers or rooted cuttings into the garden after all danger of frost, mulching the plants when they have started to grow. Staking is also advisable.

For prize-winning blooms, space plants 3 ft. apart, and dig a planting hole for each plant to a depth of 12 in., filling it with good garden compost, well-decomposed animal manure, bone meal or a packaged bulb fertilizer, placing the root 5 in. deep in the hole.

In fall after frost has killed off the foliage, the tubers can be lifted and stored through the winter in a cool, slightly humid place at 40 degrees, although they are not easy to keep, since too dry an atmosphere will shrivel them up and too moist an atmosphere will turn them to jelly.

The most popular classes of dahlias are the formal and informal decorative, cactus and pompon types. Specialist dahlia growers offer hundreds of named varieties.

Gladiolus

Gladiolus nana. The most popular cut flower in America is considered to be the gladiolus, a tall stately summer-flowering bulb growing 5 ft. in height. Large flowering-size bulbs (or corms) will flower within 70 days of planting after danger of frost, depending on variety. They need full sun and a well-drained, fertile soil, requiring conditions similar to dahlias. In exposed places plants will need staking.

Although gladiolus corms will often survive the winter in protected positions, they are tender, and in northern states it is advisable to lift them in the fall after the first frost, removing bulblets and soil. Then store in a dry, airy, frost-free place until the following spring. The small bulblets will generally reach flowering size the third year if a feeding of bone meal or flower fertilizer is given each spring. Set corms at least 6 in. apart and cover with 6 in. of soil.

Dahlia Golden Heart

Gladiolus Salmon Queen

Canna (Indian Shot)

Hardy Amaryllis
Tigridia (Tiger Flower)

Color range is extensive — including green and many beautiful bicolors and pastel shades — but no blues. All-America Selections introduces lovely new varieties each year, and specialist gladiolus growers offer hundreds of named varieties. When buying gladiolus corms be careful of special cut-rate "bargain" offers. These are generally small-size bulbs measuring only 1 in. across (beware of "circumference" sizes), and these need an extra growing season to grow large enough for flowering.

Ranunculus

Ranunculus asiaticus. These relatives of anemones appear to have petals made of crepe paper. They never fail to draw admiring crowds at spring flower shows, and florists use them extensively as cut flowers. Unfortunately, they are somewhat tender, and except in coastal areas of California and southern states they are not reliably hardy. Where winters are mild they can be planted outside from October to February for blooming in early spring year after year.

In other areas of the United States, they are best raised in 6 in. pots in a cold frame or else planted 3 weeks before the last frost date in early spring, to a depth of 3 in. in rich, well-drained soil in a sunny location. They require plenty of moisture in the early stages of growth for flowering in June.

The double, globular, papery flowers are brilliantly colored in yellow, orange, red, pink and white. The tubers are claw-shaped and should be planted with points facing down. In northern states these tubers should be lifted in September after the foliage dies down and stored indoors over winter.

Tigridia

Tigridia Pavonia (Tiger flower). Beautiful three-petaled flowers with a central cup-shaped area that is generally spotted or freckled. Growing 15 in. tall, the corms are best planted in spring after danger of frost for blooming in midsummer. The color range includes white, yellow, red and pink.

Tender in northern climates, they are best treated like gladiolus and lifted each fall, storing the corms indoors in dry vermiculite or peat moss.

Tigridias prefer a well-drained, fertile soil, slightly sandy. They look best planted in groups of 6 to 12 corms, set 3 in. deep and 6 in. apart. It's also possible to grow them from seed, treating them as annuals, but sowing them early indoors in February or March to get good-size transplants.

Other Summer-Flowering Bulbs

Tuberous begonias, caladiums and garden lilies are sometimes classified as summer-flowering bulbs.

Ranunculus in full flower at the Los Angeles Arboretum

Clematis and Other Colorful Vines

Clematis paniculata

No other hardy perennial vine is capable of providing such a spectacular density of color as clematis, some varieties producing individual blooms up to 6 inches across. Well-grown specimens create such an abundance of blooms that they completely hide the foliage. Grow them up posts, by the side of a porch, along chain link fencing, up a trellis or over an arbor, and the effect in June is guaranteed to be spellbinding — providing you observe some simple cultural requirements.

Essentially, they like their heads in the sun and their feet in the shade. Set the root crown 2 to 3 inches below the soil surface in a deeply dug, rich loose soil. Planting can be done in fall or spring. Good drainage and at least 5 hours of sun a day are essential, although the roots prefer permanent shade since they enjoy a cool soil. Where there is any danger of drought during summer months, a mulch is advisable. Planted in groups or rows, they should be spaced 3 to 4 feet apart, and will grow upwards to 8 or 10 feet.

The most widely grown variety is a very old hybrid called *Jackmanii*, a huge single-flowered purple, and the largest flowered of all. *Jackmanii* was introduced in 1863 by a British nurseryman called Jackman. However, *Nelly Moser*, a large pale blue with pink petal stripes, is considered by clematis connoisseurs as the most spectacular of all varieties, introduced by the French firm of Moser, at Versailles, in 1897. With roses and flowering annuals, new varieties enjoy their widest popularity in the first years of introduction, and the old-fashioned varieties give way to new forms developed by breeders. With clematis, however, it seems they gain respect with age. *Vivyan Pennell*, a gigantic double-flowered blue, is the most handsome of the unusual double-flowered varieties.

Famous for its fragrance is *Clematis paniculata*, producing myriads of tiny bright white flowers in September on vigorous vines.

Above *Clematis* Crimson Star, *one of the best red varieties, is best pruned by thinning out.*

Left *Clematis* Henryi, *large-flowered white, generally needs only light pruning.*

Above *Clematis* Vivyan Pennell, *double-flowered lilac-blue requires little pruning.*

Left *Clematis* Jackmanii, *the most popular variety, has vigorous growth and generally needs heavy pruning in early spring.*

Canary Creeper

Tropaeolum peregrinum. Best treated as a hardy annual, 10 ft. tall, producing beautiful cut foliage and bright yellow flowers, which resemble tiny birds in flight. Related to nasturtiums. Easy to grow from seed. Prefers slight shade.

Cobaea

Cobaea scandens. Tender perennial, best treated as an annual, 8 ft. tall, flowering summer to fall. Vigorous, fast-growing climber, easily grown from seed. Produces unusual purple bell-shaped flowers. Sow indoors in pots or outdoors after danger of frost, giving it a sunny location.

Cypress Vine

Quamoclit pennata. Hardy annual, growing to 10 ft. tall, and producing delicate, finely-cut foliage and small star-shaped trumpet flowers in white, red and pink. Easy to grow from seed. Flowers all summer in sun or light shade.

Moonflower

Calonyction aculeatum. Although truly a perennial in southern states, moonflowers are best grown as annuals over most of the United States, reaching 15 ft. and producing enormous 6-in. pure white trumpet-shaped blooms that open in the late afternoon during August and September, and stay open until noon the following day.

The flowers often open with such suddenness you can actually see the petals move. Sow seeds outdoors in May after danger of frost or indoors in March to get good-size transplants for earlier blooms.

Morning Glory

Ipomoea tricolor. Tender annual, climbing to 8 ft., and blooming from midsummer to fall. Likes full sun and withstands long periods of heat and drought.

Its best use is as a quick-growing, colorful vine for arbors, fences and trellises. The most widely grown variety is *Heavenly Blue,* with large sky-blue flowers measuring up to 5 in. across. Outstanding All-America winners include *Pearly Gates,* a shiny white, *Scarlett O'Hara,* a bright rosy-red and *Early Call Rose,* a superb, early giant-flowered carmine-red with white throat.

Seed of morning glories is extremely hard, and to insure good germination, it is advisable to chip the seed coat with a sharp knife in order to allow moisture to penetrate, or soak for 24 hours in water. Sow directly into the garden after danger of frost or start indoors to get healthy young plants ready for transplanting.

Passion Vine

Passiflora incarnata. Tender perennial, growing to 10 ft., and flowering August and September. Large, waxy white flowers have purple markings and an intricate arrangement of anthers, stamens and styles, forming a conspicuous crown in the center.

These exotic flowers can be cut and floated in a dish of water

Cypress Vine

Morning Glory, Heavenly Blue

Passion vine in flower

Thunbergia (Black-eyed Susan vine)
Close-up of Trumpet Creeper blooms

to form an attractive table centerpiece.

Needs a sunny location close to the house and heavy mulching in cold areas to get it through the winter. Plants in pots can be moved indoors to a sunny room and kept as flowering indoor plants. Nursery-grown plants are generally available for outdoor planting, or seeds can be started indoors in January or February for transplanting outside after all danger of frost.

Thunbergia

Thunbergia alata (Black-eyed Susan vine). Best treated as an annual, 5 ft. high, flowering July until fall frosts. In addition to forming a quick-growing vine trained up a trellis, thunbergia makes an interesting hanging basket or container plant, and can be used as a ground cover. The white, yellow and orange flowers grow more profusely in semishade. Easily grown from seed.

Trumpet Creeper

Campsis radicans. Hardy perennial, capable of climbing to heights of 30 ft., and flowering July to September. Flowers are a brilliant orange-scarlet, trumpet-shaped in clusters, and highly attractive to hummingbirds.

Can be grown as a dense hedge if given stout supports, and there is a yellow variety. Prefers a rich, moist soil in full sun and vigorous pruning each year to keep it within bounds.

Sow the bean-size seeds outdoors from May to August or indoors anytime to gain good size transplants. When grown as a hedge, space 4 ft. apart.

Other Valuable Climbers	
Climbing nasturtiums	annual
Ornamental gourds	annual
Climbing roses	perennial
Sweet peas (tall types)	annual

Above left *Vinca minor, an evergreen ground cover, can tolerate dry conditions in shade. The blue flowers appear in spring before the leaves create excessive shade.*

Above right *Caladiums are excellent for moist shady areas. Grown from bulbs, the heart-shaped leaves are colorful all summer.*

Left *Impatiens,* Elfin Orchid, *planted against a redwood fence which affords sunlight for only a few hours in the afternoon.*

Brightening Up That Shady Corner

Most homes in cities and suburbs do not receive the minimum of 6 hours sunshine a day to grow the more common annuals and perennials.

When deciding what to plant in a shady place, it is important to realize that there are different kinds of shade — low shade, high shade, light shade, deep shade, dry shade, moist shade, morning shade and afternoon shade. Some plants recommended for "shade" will grow only in one kind of shade, while others will tolerate a wide range of shade conditions.

By far the most successful flowering annuals for a wide range of shade conditions are impatiens, begonias and coleus. About the only two difficult shade conditions for them are deep shade caused by a dense canopy of leaves or dry shade.

The best kind of shade is a moist semishaded area, where shade is formed by a light leaf canopy creating filtered sunlight, or dappled shade.

Densely shaded areas, such as from tall evergreens or a north-facing wall, are the biggest problem, but as long as there is air circulation and ventilation the problem can be solved.

Densely shaded areas can sometimes be improved. For example, if overhead tree limbs are the cause, they can often be thinned out to allow light penetration without spoiling the trees. A dark fence or cinderblock wall can be painted with a white gloss to improve the light exposure. Small beds can be mulched with alumnium foil to help improve the light intensity, especially for impatiens and begonias, which will like the cool soil insulation the aluminum foil will provide.

Unquestionably the most useful plants for deep shade are ferns, of which there are evergreen and perennial kinds. So long as the soil is deeply cultivated and enriched with moisture-holding decomposed organic material, such as garden compost, leaf mold, peat moss or animal manure, they can bring a cool serene beauty to the most difficult shade locations.

Recommended varieties are the evergreen Christmas Fern (*polystichum acrostichoides*), growing dark green fronds averaging 2 ft. in height; Maidenhair Fern (*Adiantum pedatum*), growing slender medium green fronds from spring until fall to a height of 2 ft.; Lady Fern (*Athyrium filixfemina*), making a beautiful ground cover for shady slopes growing to 3 ft.; and the tall, vigorous Ostrich Fern (*Pteretis nodulosa*), growing to 4 ft. tall.

Hostas, too, seem to tolerate excessive amounts of shade, creating a uniform ground cover with lovely purple flower spikes in summer. The white and green variegated kind (*Hosta variegata*) is especially desirable, and these are best planted as a border at the edge of a wooded area. If all of these fail, about the only alternative may be a decorative mulch such as pine needles.

Another kind of shade problem is on wooded lots of deciduous trees, where dense shade persists during summer, but the light exposure increases significantly in winter and early spring when the trees are leafless. This is an ideal environment for a "wildflower" garden, using primulas and native wildflower species which will grow, flower and even set seed before the trees block out the light with a dense canopy of foliage. (See section on wildflower gardens.)

Shade Tolerant Plants

Name	Type	Flowering	Main Use
Ageratum	tender annual	summer	edging
Ajuga	perennial	spring	ground cover
Alyssum	hardy annual	summer	edging
Anchusa	perennial, annual	summer	borders
Astilbe	perennial	summer	borders
Aubretia	perennial	spring	rock garden
Balsam	annual	summer	beds, borders
Begonia, Tuberous	tender perennial	summer	bedding, containers
Begonia, Wax	annual	summer	borders, containers
Bleeding Heart (Dicentra)	perennial	spring	borders
Bloodroot	perennial	spring	wild gardens
Browallia	tender annual	summer	borders, containers
Caladium	perennial bulb	summer	borders, containers
Canterbury Bells	biennial	summer	borders
Clarkia	tender annual	summer	borders
Cleome	tender annual	summer	beds, borders
Coleus	tender annual	summer	beds, borders
Columbine	perennial	spring	beds, borders
Coral Bells (Heuchera)	perennial	spring	beds, borders
Crocus	perennial bulb	spring	borders
Daffodil	perennial bulb	spring	beds, borders
Day lily	perennial	summer	borders
Eranthus (Aconite)	perennial bulb	spring	borders, naturalizing
Ferns	perennial	spring, summer	borders
Forget-me-not	perennial, annual	spring	beds, borders
Foxglove (Digitalis)	biennial	summer	borders
Hosta	perennial	summer	borders
Hyacinth	perennial bulb	spring	borders
Impatiens	tender annual	summer	beds, borders
Lilium (Garden Lily)	perennial	summer	borders
Lythrum	perennial	summer	borders
Mertensia (Bluebells)	perennial	spring	wild gardens
Monarda	perennial	summer	borders
Pachysandra	perennial	evergreen	ground cover
Pansy	biennial	spring	beds, borders
Periwinkle (Vinca)	annual	summer	beds, borders
Polyanthus	perennial	spring	beds, borders
Primrose	perennial	spring	borders
Siberian Squill	perennial bulb	spring	borders
Snapdragon	annual	spring, fall	beds, borders
Snowdrop	perennial bulb	spring	borders, naturalizing
Trillium	perennial	spring	wild garden
Violet	perennial	spring	borders, wild gardens
Wishbone flower (Torenia)	annual	summer	borders

Begonia Power

Top left. Hanging basket begonias are a special class developed so they cascade naturally from containers.

Top right Tuberous begonias and ferns combine to make a magnificent shade garden that's easy to grow.

Left Hybrid wax begonias Scarletta (red) and Viva (white) create a spectacular checkerboard at Longwood Gardens, Pennsylvania.

Begonia, Tuberous

Begonia tuberhybrida. The tuberous begonia is a versatile plant for shaded locations, making colorful beds, container plantings and hanging baskets.

Soil for these lovely flowers needs to be moist and rich in humus, which can be added to poor soils in the form of peat moss or well-decomposed animal manure.

Plants can be started indoors in seed flats or pots, and then transplanted to their permanent locations after all danger of frost, starting to flower in July and continuing non-stop until frost. The tubers can also be planted directly into their permanent positions.

Many excellent named varieties are available, including some spectacular frilled bicolors, the color range including yellow, pink, red, white and many shades except blue.

Begonia, Wax

Begonia semperflorens. Best treated as a tender annual, 6 to 10 in. tall, blooming from early summer to autumn. Flower color, often dazzling: white, pink, scarlet and red. Leaves may be green or bronze. One of the best annuals for light-to-moderate shade, hybrids also grow well in sun in all but the hottest areas. Excellent for border plantings or containers.

Compact F1 hybrids are superior to older types. *Cocktail* series, in mixed or separate colors, grows to 6 in. and has bronze leaves. *Pink Charm* and *White Charm* are taller green-leaved varieties. There are also double-flowered kinds, including *Christmas Candle,* which has rose-red blooms.

Start seed indoors early, or purchase young plants in spring. They can be increased from cuttings to make good pot plants in winter. Seed is extremely small and requires a long time to grow to good transplanting size. Handle expensive hybrid seed

Above *Coleus border planted with a fringed variety. The standard-form coleus in the background, trained like a tree and kept indoors during the winter, is pruned to a single stem.*

Right *Tall, tapering spikes of foxglove create a stunning effect in cool semishaded locations.*

with the damp end of a sharp pencil, starting indoors in January for outdoor transplanting in May.

Caladiums

These beautiful foliage plants thrive in moist shady places and grow from bulbs that can be planted directly into the garden after danger of frost or started early in seed flats and pots.

Although effective when planted as a mixture, the most spectacular display is from a named variety called *candidum* — a ghostly white with dark green veins that can make a stunning bed or border planted entirely alone. They also make attractive house plants.

Caladium bulbs can be lifted in the fall and reliably stored over winter in a cool dry place.

Coleus

Coleus Blumei. Although a perennial in warm climates, coleus is best treated as a tender annual. It is planted extensively for its colorful variegated foliage in combinations of yellow, lime green, bronze, red and chocolate. Effective all season. Thrives in sun but tolerant of part shade. Usually grows to about 1 ft.

Pinching the lead shoots after transplanting will produce a more uniform bedding effect.

Useful as a border plant, edging, or in containers. *Rainbow* (mixed colors) is ideal for mass plantings because of its broadly toothed leaves and dramatic colorings. *Carefree,* a strain available in mixed or separate colors, has distinctively frilled foliage.

Start seed indoors in a soil temperature of 70 to 75 degrees, or purchase young plants after danger of frost has passed. Desirable forms are easily rooted from cuttings and carried over winter in the home as pot plants.

Dicentra

Dicentra spectabilis (Bleeding Heart). Hardy perennial, growing to 4 ft. high, and blooming in May or June with arching stems loaded with pink pendant heart-shaped blooms. Best grown from plants since seed takes up to 50 days to germinate. Roots can be divided in early spring and planted 18 in. apart. Plants resemble shrubs and should be used sparingly as a highlight in the perennial border or between shrubs.

Foxglove

Digitalis purpurea. Although foxgloves are really biennials, blooming the second year, then dying off, they are often mistaken for everlasting perennials since they self-seed easily.

Growing 5 ft. tall, they produce tubular flowers on a tall tapering spike, each flower handsomely freckled with contrasting spots which help to guide bees to the pollen-laden center. Basic colors are white, yellow, red, purple and pink.

The seeds are tiny and are best started indoors in July to get healthy transplants, pressing the seeds into the soil mix, but not covering. Germinate at 70 degree soil temperature for 7 days and transplant to permanent positions in September, protecting against severe winters with a straw mulch. Alternatively, seeds may be directsown into the garden in July in a cool semishaded area. Cool conditions favor foxgloves, and they will tolerate light shade. A perennial border or at the edge of trees is a favored place for them.

The most recent innovation among foxgloves is an annual variety called *Foxy,* which will

Above left Hosta variegata *in full flower likes moist shade. Even when not in bloom, the leaves of this hardy perennial are decorative.*

Above right *Wishbone flower* (torenia fournieri) *will flower as an annual in a wide range of soil conditions, where shade is not too dense.*

Left *Helleborus, an early spring-flowering perennial, likes moist shade, particularly under deciduous trees.*

bloom in 5 months from sowing the seed. The plant is shorter than the perennial kind, averaging 2-1/2 ft., and it will produce a second showing of blooms the following season.

In medicine the dried leaves are noted for a drug called digitalis, which slows down the heart and can be fatal unless properly administered under the control of a doctor.

Helleborus

Helleborus niger (Christmas Rose). Hardy perennial, 15 in. high, used in borders for early spring blooms, even before many early-flowering bulbs are in bloom. The waxy flowers resemble anemones and make attractive flower arrangements. They thrive best in a cool, moist, position and in a soil rich in organic matter, such as peat moss or leaf mold. Best situation is a place that is shaded by trees in summer, but exposed to sun in winter, such as under deciduous trees. Colors include white, purple (*orientalis*) and green (*corsicus*). Best grown from plants set out in spring or fall, since seed germination is slow and takes 3 years to bloom.

Hosta

Hardy perennials, forming thick clumps of leaves 18 in. high, followed in summer by long spikes topped with lilac bell-shaped flowers. They will thrive in shade where few other plants can survive.

Does best in a moist, fertile soil, but tolerates a wide range of soil conditions. Creates a good ground cover when left to its own devices and looks especially attractive against a hedge or at the edge of trees.

Hosta variegata is a recommended variety for perennial borders and for edgings, growing light green leaves that are variegated silvery white. Grow from root divisions in spring or fall.

Impatiens

Impatiens walleriana. Tender annual, 6 in. to 2 ft., blooming early summer to autumn. Queen of the shade-loving plants, impatiens has come a long way since breeders learned to create hybrids among them. New varieties appear every year. The color range includes white,

orange, pink, rose, red and bicolors. There are dwarf, medium and tall types.

Excellent for edgings and borders. Also makes a good indoor pot plant. Recommended series: *Elfin* (6 to 12 in.) and *Imp* (1 to 2 ft.).

Sow seed early indoors for best results or purchase seedlings after danger of frost has passed. Choice color forms are easily propagated by cuttings. Seed germinates best at 65 to 70 degrees. Provide plenty of moisture, preferably with a fine spray.

Torenia

Torenia fournieri (Wishbone flower). Tender annual, 12 in. high, flowering June to October. Flowers are deep blue and yellow, shaped like tiny pansies with a conspicuous "wishbone" in the center.

Excellent for beds with semishade, torenia are long-lasting, and easy to grow from seed sown indoors March 1st, then transplanted to permanent locations. Outdoors they can be sown in May.

Primula vulgaris (*English primrose*) brightens up shady areas in early spring.

Polyanthus Pacific Giant *is the earliest to grow from seed and makes exquisite pot plants.*

Primroses and Polyanthus

One of the most uplifting sights of early spring is the sight of primroses (primulas) and polyanthus bursting into glorious bloom in beds and borders and under still leafless trees.

A question constantly asked is: "What is the difference between primulas and polyanthus?" Basically primulas are selections of wild species such as *Primula vulgaris* (wild primrose,) *Primula veris* (cowslip) and *Primula japonica* (candelabra primulas). The parentage of polyanthus is essentially a man-made cross between the wild primrose and *Primula variabilis,* which in itself is a cross between the wild primrose and the cowslip.

Primulas themselves have widely differing needs since there are more than 300 known species. For example, the wild primrose enjoys a habitat in deeply shaded woodland, while the cowslip grows with wild abandon in open meadowland, and the candelabra primulas demand boggy wet ground.

As a result of its ancestry, polyanthus is more widely adapted than any of the primulas. It meets difficulty only in deep shade where it produces too much leaf growth and too little bloom, and in dry, exposed areas where its demands for moisture cannot be satisfied.

Biggest failures growing polyanthus from seed are generally attributed to lack of moisture. If the seed bed or seed flat is allowed to dry out for as short a time as 2 hours the plants will perish.

Correct time to sow seeds is September, sprinkling the tiny seed thinly in a seed flat or planter filled with a moist planting medium, then barely covering the seed with fine soil. Seed germinates in 20 days, and the seedlings will need to be thinned to 5 inches apart or transplanted to individual pots and protected in a cold frame during winter.

The seedlings should be planted out into the garden in April or May, during a spell of damp weather, spaced 10 inches apart. A soil that is enriched with organic matter such as peat moss, garden compost, leafmold or decomposed manure suits polyanthus best, and for this reason, they make excellent companion plants for early blooming varieties of rhododendrons and azaleas.

Polyanthus grow slowly from outdoor sowing, which is why nurseries and garden centers each spring do a steady business in them. Grown indoors this time span can be condensed to 7 months with the new hybrids such as *Pacific Giants.* Under artificial lights or in a greenhouse, they can be kept indoors to flower as pot plants and then transferred to the garden after blooming indoors.

Primula auricula, *a hardy alpine suitable for sunny rock gardens, forms color rings of purple, red, green, yellow and brown.*

Cowslips (Primula veris) *prefer a more open, sunny location than other primroses.*

Polyanthus and rhododendrons make good companions, thriving together in similar soil and shade conditions.

Rhododendrons—
King of the Shade Garden

Azalea Mollis

It may seem strange to single out rhododendrons from the vast numbers of flowering shrubs, but to talk about shade gardens and *not* make some mention of the value of rhododendrons would be a grave oversight.

Best of all, rhododendrons like high shade — a location which is shaded by tall trees through which filtered light penetrates, but they will do well wherever there is free air circulation and an acid humus-rich soil. Where there are no trees, the north or west side of a house, fence or high hedge is also suitable.

A familiar question among home gardeners is: "What's the difference between a rhododendron and an azalea?" The answer is there is no real difference — azaleas botanically are really rhododendrons, but nurserymen like to classify them separately, calling those plants with broad leaves rhododendrons and those with narrow leaves azaleas.

The most exotic of all the azaleas are the Kurume hybrids, growing 3 to 5 feet tall and creating such a dense floral display, they completely hide the foliage in spring. They are easily pruned and extensively used in Japanese-style gardens, in bold sweeps of color along walks, on slopes and at the edge of lawns or trees.

The Exbury hybrid azaleas, forming large flower trusses, were developed by Lord Rothschild of the famous banking firm. When you buy a special selection from these called the "Supremes," each plant has a statement of authenticity from Lionel de Rothschild, who inherited the family's love of gardening as well as its wealth. They are rich in yellow and orange, as well as whites, lavenders and pinks, and a border of all the colors is a glorious sight in spring.

Books have been written on rhododendrons alone, and some men have been fired with so much enthusiasm for collecting them, they have risked life and limb in the mountains of China and Tibet to find new species or have financed explorers to do the collecting for them.

I have yet to find a rhododendron that gives more universal pleasure than *America,* a brilliant red variety with large trusses. For wild gardens, *Rhododendron canescens,* the Piedmont azalea, is a breathtaking sight covered in clusters of dainty blush-white trumpet-shaped blossoms.

How to Plant a Rhododendron

The most successful method of planting rhododendrons (or azaleas) is to buy young shrubs that are "balled and burlapped." They cost more than bare-root trees, but they are almost "idiot-proof." They have been dug from the nursery with a good size root ball and then wrapped in burlap sacking to keep the soil well packed around the roots. Take your rhododendrons home, then follow these steps:

1 — Plant rhododendrons where they will not need pruning. Although they can be pruned, you will generally lose the following year's blossoms by doing so.

2 — Dig a hole at least 1-1/2 feet deep by 1-1/2 feet wide.

3 — Carefully unwrap the burlap around the root ball, disturbing as little soil as possible around the roots. Fill the hole to half its depth with a mixture of garden soil, compost and peat moss. Pour a bucket of water over this and set the tree on top of it so the top of the root ball is level with the top of the hole.

4 — Keeping the plant centered in the hole, fill the top half of the hole with a mixture of garden soil and peat moss, leaving a one inch lip around the edge to catch water. Pour in another bucket of water and tread the soil down firmly.

5 — Spread a decorative pine bark mulch around the roots.

With bare-root rhododendrons you can follow the same procedure. Before planting, however, soak the roots for at least half a day in water, trimming off any broken roots.

Step 1   Step 2   Step 3   Step 4

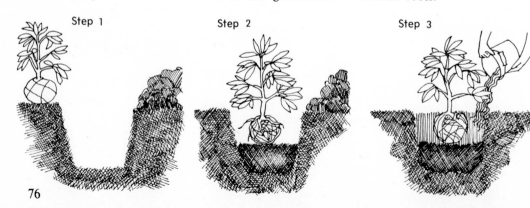

Left *Azalea mollis grows the purest yellow flowers and is sweetly scented.*

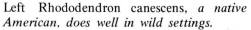

Above *Rhododendron* America, *one of the finest of all rhododendrons*

Above *One of the best blue rhododendrons is* Blue Peter.

Left Rhododendron canescens, *a native American, does well in wild settings.*

Above *Rhododendron* Boule de Neige *is perhaps the finest of all white-flowered rhododendrons.*

Left *Miniature azalea garden like this could fit into almost anyone's backyard.*

Beautiful rock garden shows good balance between foliage plants and flowering plants.

Rock Gardens and Plants for Dry Places

The finest rock gardens incorporate three essential natural elements — plants, rocks and water. There is perhaps no greater challenge in gardening than to work these three gifts of nature into a naturalistic, harmonious landscape — an art at which the Japanese are masters.

The best site for a rock garden is a slope facing southwest in an exposed position, not shaded or overhung with trees. The side of a pond is perfect, but not essential, and although a cascading water course is desirable, it can be excluded if cost and effort are to be saved.

Good drainage is most important in selecting the site, since rock plants will not tolerate water-laden soil around their roots, especially in winter.

Any size is possible — from miniature rock gardens created in enamel or concrete containers, planted with bonsai and dwarf alpine plants, to whole hillsides complete with stepping stone pathways, evergreens, boulders, rustic bridges, cascading waterfalls and rock pools filled with fish and miniature water lilies.

Stone is the prime requisite, and in selecting stone it is generally a good policy to use a local stone. This is likely to be least expensive and create a more natural look for your garden. Avoid using small stones. Pieces weighing up to 100 pounds can be carried single-handed or in a wheelbarrow. A few larger boulders, using an assistant to lift into place, are also desirable as highlights. Figure on needing one ton of stone per 100 square feet of rock garden.

Soil preparation should be done before stones are set into place. Dig over the site and remove all subsoil obstructions, such as weed roots and trash. Build up from this your desired slope and shape, using a mixture of 3 parts good topsoil, 1-1/2 parts peat moss and 1-1/2 parts sharp sand.

Start laying rocks at ground level, gradually building up bluffs, outcrops and stepping stones. Cluster rocks in groups rather than spacing them evenly over a wide area. Set every stone firmly in place with the broadest side buried and sloping backwards at the same "tilt" as other rocks in order to create harmony. As each outcrop is completed, fill it level with soil. Crevices which are to contain plants should be packed firmly with soil, leaving no air pockets.

A good rock garden will feature a balance of perennial and evergreen plant material, ensuring some form of color all year round. Dwarf evergreens, spreading juniper, dwarf azaleas, dwarf rhododendrons, sempervivums, hardy prickly pear cactus, heathers and evergreen ferns are essential for the "backbone" and to give the garden character and form during winter months. For earliest blooms, flowering bulbs are essential, especially clumps of crocus, snowdrops, *Fritillaria Meleagris,* miniature daffodils and "water lily" tulips belonging to the Kaufmanniana class. Miniature *Iris reticulata* are also exquisite.

Best of the early-flowering rock garden perennials are *Alyssum saxatile,* ajuga, arabis, armeria, alpine aster, aubretia and *Phlox subulata.* For summer beauty, best of the bunch are astilbe, artemisia, candytuft, cerastium, dianthus (pinks), gypsophila, helianthemum, miniature roses and *Sedum spectabile.*

Yucca is a valuable hardy evergreen perennial, producing stiff sword-shaped leaves with a tropical appearance. In mid-summer a large flower stem resembling a giant asparagus spear appears from the center of each clump and opens up into a plume of waxy white flowers. Tolerates a wide range of soils, especially dry soils in full sun. Best grown from plants.

Sempervivums are hardy succulent plants, forming fleshy rosettes in a wide variety of colors, many bicolored. Excellent for planting on dry walls, in crevices on boulders, on pieces of driftwood. In a dry, warm, sunny location many types will also produce interesting flower spikes. Commonly called "Hen and Chickens" because mature plants will surround themselves with young off-shoots. Best grown from plants.

Prickly pear is a hardy perennial cactus that generally falls limp in winter, but revives in spring to carpet the ground with prickly pads and exotic yellow flowers, followed by deep red fruits. Best grown from plants. There are many other varieties of tender prickly pear cactus suitable for growing outdoors in desert areas.

It can be a problem deciding what to plant on expansive dry slopes, especially if you'd like something colorful. Crownvetch has become extremely popular. Planted from crowns or seeds, it creates a bushy, spreading plant with pink pea-shaped flowers. Also worth consideration is perennial sweet pea, or lathyrus, growing dense vines with white and pink flowers resembling sweet peas. Both lathyrus and crownvetch are good for erosion control and last indefinitely without getting out of hand.

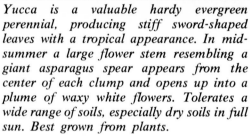

Rock Garden Ideas

Pockets for rock plants

Stones set to slope down

Ground level

Island-type rock garden on a flat site with good drainage

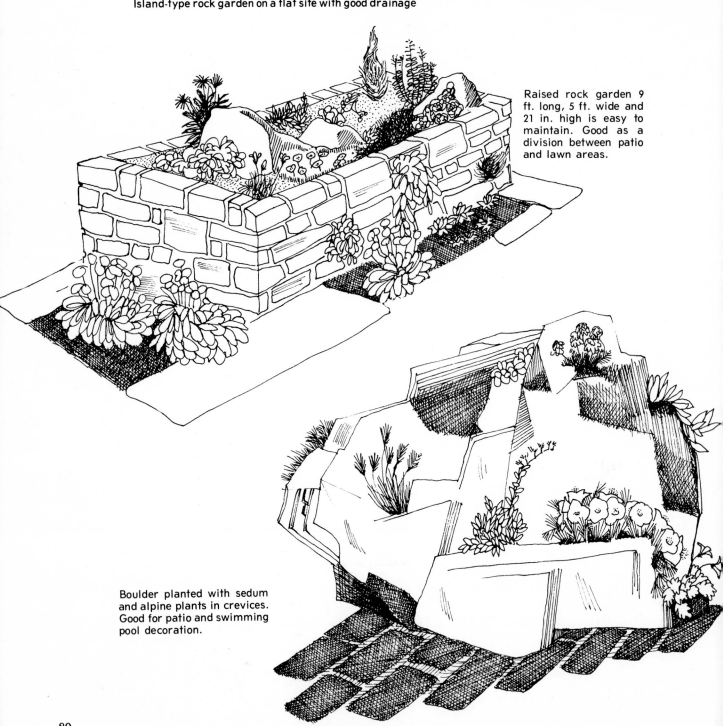

Raised rock garden 9 ft. long, 5 ft. wide and 21 in. high is easy to maintain. Good as a division between patio and lawn areas.

Boulder planted with sedum and alpine plants in crevices. Good for patio and swimming pool decoration.

Japanese rock garden featuring azaleas, ferns and dwarf bamboo, plus boulders and running water

Simple but colorful backyard rock garden featuring candytuft (white) and perennial (yellow) alyssum. Also in flower are bergenia, a hardy perennial, displaying tall pink flower spikes and broad leaves, and aethionema, a pink-flowered ground-hugging hardy perennial.

Best Flowers for Rock Gardens

Alyssum (annual and perennial)
Arabis (perennial)
Armeria (perennial)
Aster, Alpine (perennial)
Aubretia (perennial)
Brachycombe (annual)
California-poppy (annual)
Candytuft (perennial)
Cerastium (perennial)
Chionodoxa (flowering bulb)
Crocus (flowering bulb)
Daffodil, Miniature (flowering bulb)
Dianthus (perennial)
Dimorphotheca (annual)
Eranthis (flowering bulb)
Forget-Me-Not (perennial)
Gazania (annual)

Helianthemum (perennial)
Heuchera (perennial)
Iris reticulata (flowering bulb)
Lobelia (annual)
Lunaria (perennial)
Phlox, Creeping (perennial)
Portulaca (annual)
Rose, Miniature (perennial)
Sedum (perennial)
Sempervivums (perennial)
Siberian Squill (flowering bulb)
Snowdrops (flowering bulb)
Triteleia (flowering bulb)
Tulip chrysantha (flowering bulb)
Tulip dasystemon (flowering bulb)
Tulip kaufmanniana (flowering bulb)
Verbena (annual)

Best Flowers for Dry Slopes

Ajuga (perennial)
Armeria (perennial)
Daffodils (flowering bulb)
Day lily (perennial)
Iris, Bearded

Penngift Crownvetch (perennial)
Perennial Sweet Pea (perennial)
Phlox, Creeping (perennial)
Prickly Pear
Yucca

Plants for Wet and Moist Places

Water Lilies

When summer temperatures hit the 90's and the humidity hangs heavy in the air, what could be more soothing than to relax by your own garden pool with water lilies and have lazy goldfish take food from your fingers?

Water Lilies

Basically, there are two kinds of water lilies: the hardies and the tropicals. The hardies can be planted in May and will bloom within a month under good conditions, continuing on until made dormant by frost. Being perennials, they winter well in the pool. Colors are mainly white, yellow and shades of red. Their chief enemies are ducks and water rats, which relish the young shoots. A covering of wire mesh, such as chickenwire molded over the mouth of a container, can add protection.

Tropical water lilies are more exotic than the hardies, with larger leaves and much larger flowers. They bloom in a wider range of colors — including blue — and all are deliciously fragrant. But they are more

trouble. In all but frost-free areas, they must be replanted every year, since they will not survive the winter. They are classified as day-blooming and night-blooming varieties. The night bloomers open at dusk and remain open until noon the following day. They are an exquisite sight seen by the full moon or by outdoor floodlights.

It's best to plant your water lily roots in containers filled with 12 quarts of rich garden soil and then sink the container in the pool where you want them to bloom. The growing points should show through the soil and should be submerged under 16 inches of water. To maintain this depth, you may have to prop up the container with stones or bricks. For the winter, these containers should be lowered to the pool floor so they are below the ice line. With shallow pools, remove the containers to a cool frost-free basement and keep moist. To produce their best blooms, water lilies require plenty of sunlight (at least 6 hours a day). They like still water and fertile soil. Given these three basic essentials, you can leave them to their own devices with no hoeing, weeding or watering necessary on your part!

Water lily Marliac White *is the largest-flowered of hardy white water lilies.*

Water lily Helvola *grows flowers barely bigger than a dollar piece on plants that spread one foot.*

Other Perennial Water Plants

To make a garden pool more natural, you should consider adding other flowering perennial water plants, planting them in submerged containers to keep them within bounds.

Lotus

A breathtaking sight in the water garden and good companions to water lilies. Held sacred in the Orient and Middle East, they are symbols of fertility in Egypt. The blossoms measure up to 16 in. across on 9-foot stems. The leaves look like parasols, the fragrance is haunting, and there is something mysterious and prehistoric about the gigantic seed pods which rattle when shaken and are prized by flower arrangers.

Lotus plants prefer a heavy soil containing 25 per cent clay and plenty of organic fertilizer, such as well-decomposed cow manure. They grow similar to hardy water lilies and will survive the winter, if the roots can be kept clear of the ice line.

Arrowhead

(*Sagittaria latifolia*). Has shapely, attractive dark green leaves that are arrow-shaped and a welcome change from the usual lance-leaf or round-shaped leaves of water plants. Growing upright to 3 ft. in height, they produce an attractive white flower spike in summer. Spreading by runners, the roots can be planted in marshy soil with up to 6 in. of water above them.

Cattails

(*Typha latifolia*). These are known throughout Europe as "bullrushes". Their handsome dark brown poker-shaped flower heads or "tails" fluff out into wind-blown seed heads by fall. Growing 5 to 6 ft. tall, they thrive in 1 to 6 in. of water and reproduce so rapidly from creeping rootstocks it is essential to confine them to a submerged container.

Victoria Regia

Makes a spectacular sight when you have space for them. They form huge round water lily pads with upturned edges. These leaves are so big and bouyant that they can support the weight of a small child. Huge white flowers bloom at night with the fragrance of a pineapple, last 2 days, and undergo a remarkable color change by turning to pink, then purple. Growing requirements are the same as other water lilies.

Water Iris

(*Iris Pseudacorus*). Grows 2 to 3 ft. high with lovely yellow and blue flowers appearing in May. The lance-like leaves are attractive all through the season. Plant the root crowns under 2 in. of water.

Water Poppies

(*Limnocharis Humboldtii*). Are especially appealing, bearing bright yellow 3-petalled flowers with contrasting chocolate-brown markings. The plants spread low over the water in neat clumps, producing masses of flowers in summer. Plant roots up to 10 in. below the surface in a submerged container.

Lotus blossom pictured in the Aquatic Gardens, Washington D.C.

Victoria Regia *lily pads will often support the weight of a small child.*

Water gardens need not be large, and it's easy to have your own — so easy in fact that you can build one yourself over a weekend.

Water lily pools can be created in a wide range of shapes and sizes from the small weekend-made pool to large farm ponds. An ideal size for the average small garden or patio is 2-1/2 feet deep, by 3 feet wide, by 5 feet long. The secret is to use a tough, flexible plastic liner instead of the usual concrete. Just excavate the pool to the desired shape and depth, lining it with a layer of sand or sifted soil. Then stretch the pool liner taut over the hole, anchor it with bricks or stones spaced around the edges, and fill it with water from a hose. The weight of water keeps the liner down, holding it to the shape of your hole.

Remove the weights from the edge and then cover the flaps along the side with a neat border of crazy paving. It's that simple, and you have a water garden that's ready to be stocked right away with lovely water lilies and a host of other fascinating water-loving plants. If this sounds like too much of a project for you, water lilies can be grown in attractive wooden tubs.

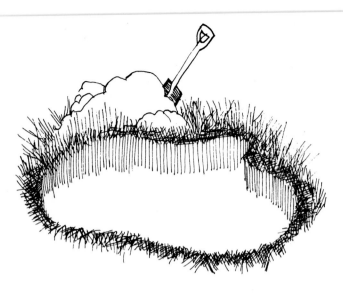

1. Mark out shape of your pool and remove soil to depth of 1½ to 2 ft.

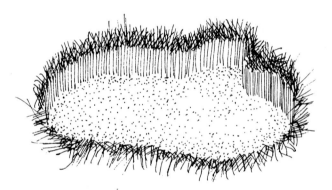

2. Put down a layer of sand or newspapers to cushion weight of the water and prevent liner damage.

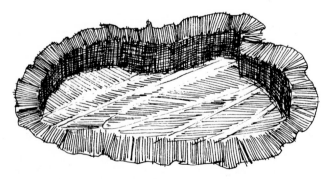

3. Lay liner in the hole, neatly folding liner at edges of pool to take up any slack. Heavy gauge black plastic or polyethelene is ideal.

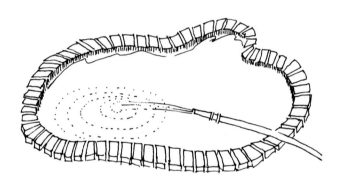

4. Fill pool with water and use heavy bricks or slabs to hide and weight down liner.

5. Plant water lilies in tubs filled with heavy garden soil and compost. For lotus use the same type of soil, but with about one quarter clay.

Plants for Moist Places

In addition to plants that will grow *in* water, there is another group of valuable flowering perennials that require permanently moist soil such as found at the side of streams and ponds. They cannot tolerate being entirely submerged in water like water lilies and other water plants, but they will do well where a marshy or boggy condition persists all year.

Candelabra Primulas

(*Primula japonica*). Just one of a vast number of primulas which are bog-loving plants, they are by far the most spectacular and the easiest to grow, flowering in May and June. The leaf clusters form dense low-growing rosettes that send up 2 ft. stems topped by a dome of primrose-shaped flowers in shades of red with contrasting "eyes". They thrive by the side of streams and ponds in semishade where the soil is permanently moist and rich in organic matter, such as leaf mold or peat moss. Plants can be propagated by root division, and flowers reseed readily.

Hardy Hibiscus

(*Hibiscus Moscheutos*). There are several popular types of hardy hibiscus which are equally at home in the perennial border and in a cool, moist soil; but the most spectacular of these is unquestionably a new variety developed in Japan called *Southern Belle,* an All-America award winner.

Southern Belle can be treated as a hardy annual, blooming in late summer to fall on bushy, 5-foot tall plants. The flowers, up to 10 in. across, are white, rose and crimson with contrasting "eyes". Well-grown specimens have a striking tropical appearance, and the immense flower size never fails to amaze.

To get flowers the first year, seed must be sown indoors in February for transplanting when plants are a foot high. Jiffy-7 peat pellets are ideal for this purpose, and a temperature of 70 degrees is needed for reliable germination. After frost in fall, plants die back, and except in cold areas, they can be encouraged to make new growth the following spring by a layer of protective mulch. Thereafter they will perform as perennials.

Marsh Marigold

(*Caltha palustris*). One of the earliest waterside plants to flower in spring, creating a dense mound of fleshy green leaves covered in gleaming buttercup-yellow flowers that shimmer in the spring sunlight. Propagates itself by runners and does best when the root crown is barely below water.

Ostrich Fern

(*Pteretis nodulosa*). Needs plenty of room, since its majestic fronds will reach 4 ft. in height, but like most members of the fern family, it has a graceful beauty few other plants can match. They are vigorous growers, spread rapidly once established, and are propagated by root division. Also beautiful in springtime are the young fern fronds, or fiddleheads, as they uncurl from winter dormancy. Cinnamon fern (*Osmunda cinnamonea*) and Royal fern (*Osmunda regalis*) are less domineering than the Ostrich and equally at home in waterlogged soil that is rich in leaf mold or other organic matter.

Purple Loosetrife

(*Lythrum*). Equally at home in the perennial border or pondside, where moist conditions bring out its best. Growing to 4 ft. tall, its reddish-purple flowers appear in summer on tall tapering spikes. Plant in fall or spring and propagate from root cuttings.

Sweet Violet

(*Viola odorata*). Blooms in spring on neat mound-shaped plants so dense that they can make an effective ground cover. The purple or white fragrant blooms create a carpet of color when successfully naturalized and make dainty flower posies for indoor flower arrangements. Tolerates light shade and propagates easily from root division.

Water Forget-Me-Not

(*Myosotis palustris*). Flowers freely in spring and early summer with clusters of beautiful clear blue flowers on 9-in. plants. It naturalizes easily, self-seeds readily, and tolerates light shade. Not to be confused with the common garden forget-me-not (*Myosotis alpestris*) used extensively in spring flower beds.

Ferns thrive here in a cool, moist glen.

Candelabra Primulas naturalized by the side of a stream at the Winterthur Garden, Delaware.

Wildflowers
and Wild Gardens

Wild Violet

Spring nowhere asserts its mystical influence more dramatically than with wild flowers. The sun, penetrating the still leafless trees, warms the forest floor and gives dormant wildflowers a spurt of energy that sends them bursting into bloom within a period of days.

Flowers of skunk cabbage make the first appearance. Mottled purple and white, they almost merge with the moist brown soil in which they thrive. The flowers are soon followed by the conspicuous cabbage-green leaves which smell of skunk when cut or crushed.

The most remarkable flower in the woods is Jack-in-the-Pulpit. All young plants begin life as males. But after 3 or 4 years as males, they actually change sex and become females. In the fall fertilized females then produce clusters of brilliant red berries containing seed to propagate the species. The sex change is possible only when the plant has built up enough energy in its underground bulb. If the plant is in a poor location and cannot find sufficient nourishment, it stays male all its life. If, after becoming female, its reserves of energy are depleted, it changes back into a male. Look for Jack-in-the-Pulpit in moist shady places near streams and ponds during the first week of April.

A wild garden, planted with wildflowers and ferns, outcroppings of rock and delicately landscaped with mountain laurel around an informal lily pond fed by a sparkling stream, is the kind of garden that can be a reality. Many good nurseries and landscape designers specialize in naturalistic wild gardens, and if you prefer to design your own, you can even buy wildflowers as ready-grown plants to save you the chore of growing them from seed.

Natural gardens are highly practical. Once established, they tend to take care of themselves, seem immune from disease, and improve in beauty from year to year. America abounds with places to see examples of wild gardens and observe close-up the nation's rich bounty of wildflowers.

Your wildflower garden can be as simple or ambitious as you wish to make it. It can be as small as any other flower bed consisting merely of a small rock garden in a shady corner or a bed of ferns. Or it could take in several acres complete with streams and waterfalls, rustic bridges, bridle paths, clumps of weeping willow and silver birch.

Jack-in-the-Pulpit (spring)

Jack-in-the-Pulpit (fall)

Best Wild Plants for Wild Gardens

Name	Range	Flowering Time	Comments
Arbutus	Canada to Florida	April-May	shell pink flowers; trailing
Bloodroot	Canada to Florida	April-May	white anemone-like blooms
Bluebells, Virginia	New York to S. Carolina	April-May	blue flowers like a cowslip
Bluets	Canada to Georgia	May	myriads of light blue flowers
Butterfly Weed	Maine to Florida	July-Sept.	spectacular orange flowers
Columbine, Wild	Canada to Florida	April-May	red flowers, tipped yellow
Dutchman's Breeches	Canada to N. Carolina	April-May	graceful white blossoms
Foamflower	Canada to Florida	April-May	dainty white flower spikes; ground cover
Gentian	Canada to Georgia	Aug.-Sept.	rich blue flowers
Geranium, Wild	Maine to Georgia	May-June	pink flowers
Jack-in-the-Pulpit	All states	April-May	red berries in fall
Lady's-Slipper	Canada to N. Carolina	May-June	pink orchid-like blooms; tricky also, yellow variety
Lily, Canada	Canada to Georgia	July-Aug.	deep yellow spotted flowers
Lobelia, Cardinal	All states	July-Aug.	brilliant red flower spikes
Marigold, Marsh	Canada to S. Carolina	April-May	buttercup yellow flowers
May Apple	Canada to Florida	April-May	waxy white flowers; ground cover
Shooting Star	Pennsylvania to Ga.	May	reddish-purple flowers
Solomon's Seal, false	Canada to N. Carolina	May-June	plumes of white flowers
Spring Beauty	Canada to N. Carolina	April-May	delicate pinkish-white flowers
Star of Bethlehem	All states	May	white flowers; bulbous plants
Trillium	Canada to N. Carolina	April-May	white and red kinds; three petaled
Violet, Blue	Canada to Florida	April-May	violet-blue flowers; ground cover
Violet, Dog's-Tooth (Trout Lily)	Canada to Florida	April-May	tiny yellow lily-like flowers

Bloodroot Flowers

America's wildflowers are more prolific during spring than any other time of year. Many will grow, flower, store food and make seeds even before the trees are in full leaf.

Dazzling in their brightness are flowers of Bloodroot. The anemone-like flowers are clear white and spring from a thick root that bleeds blood-red when cut.

Look for the charming Dog's-Tooth Violet, or Trout Lily, in damp shady places. Like a miniature Turk's Cap Lily, its flowers are a shining yellow.

Another early flower — perhaps the most common in all of the north is the May Apple, covering the woodland floor with pairs of huge fig-like leaves that almost hide a large waxy white flower.

Dutchman's Breeches are a lovely sight on rocky slopes in wooded areas during April. It transplants easily and combines well with ferns.

A must for every wildflower garden is the elusive Pink Lady's-slipper, which puffs out an exotic orchid-like bloom in early May. They are extremely difficult to grow from seed, but established plants can be bought from a specialist wildflower nursery.

Discover Bluets, or Quaker Ladies, at the edge of woods or open meadows. These starry-eyed blue flowers are a stunning sight, growing in masses close to the ground and creating the effect of a long ribbon of dew in the early morning.

Bluets (Quaker Ladies)

Spring Beauty

Left *Wild garden featuring arched bridge and stony creek. As with most wild gardens, dogwoods and azaleas are needed for bold color.*

Trout Lily (Erythronium)

Butterfly Weed

Trillium grandiflorum

Of all the different kinds of Trilliums, the *Giant Trillium* is by far the most beautiful. Three-petalled and white as snow, it is a quaint sight on wooded slopes and ideal for introducing into your own garden if you can provide shade and acid soil.

Virginia Bluebells, Wild Columbine, Blue Phlox, Wood Geraniums and Fiddlehead Ferns are examples of other enchanting wildflowers to grow in your garden. Watch for them in the months of April and May — spring's flush of wildflowers is a miracle of nature you should not miss.

Fiddlehead Ferns

Virginia Bluebell (*Mertensia*)

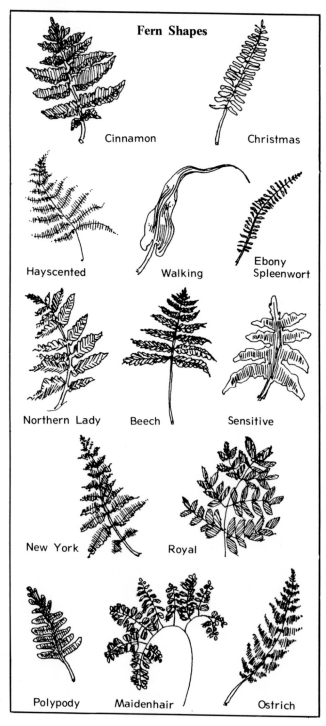

Fern Shapes

Cinnamon

Christmas

Hayscented

Walking

Ebony Spleenwort

Northern Lady

Beech

Sensitive

New York

Royal

Polypody

Maidenhair

Ostrich

Featured in this balcony garden are cascading petunias, coleus, geraniums, dusty miller, wax begonias, and variegated vinca.

Terracotta Italian ornamental urn provides a decorative setting for an all yellow theme of Dainty Marietta marigolds, dwarf dahlias, and calendulas.

Container Planting Ideas

Even among homeowners fortunate enough to have large gardens, there is generally a patio area, screened-in porch or balcony that needs a touch of color to bring the outdoors closer to the house.

Many shapes and sizes of containers can be purchased from garden centers and nurseries, but you'll find it a lot more fun to hunt for unusual containers in junk shops, antique stores, and at auctions. Rusty old kettles, cauldrons, and chipped farm troughs can be delightful "finds" and inexpensive. Bushel baskets, plastic buckets, coffee cans and other easily accessible containers are also good to use.

Soil Preparation

For gardening in containers you can purchase a soil substitute or synthetic packaged soil product readily available from nurseries and garden centers, made from a mixture of horticultural vermiculite, peat moss and fertilizer. It has some advantages over common garden soil, since it is sterile and free from disease, contains no weed seeds and generally holds moisture and plant nutrients well. Also, it's light-weight and easily handled.

A good crumbly, moisture-holding soil is the most important part of successful container gardening, but if you have access to good garden soil, it's easy to make a suitable soil mix yourself.

The best all-around do-it-yourself mix consists of two parts sieved garden soil, one part sand or perlite, and one part peat moss, leaf mold or well-decomposed animal manure.

Planting

Containers come in two kinds — those with drainage holes and those without. Small containers, such as pots and window boxes, should have drainage holes to prevent water-logging.

When a container has drainage holes, place stones or broken clay crocks over the holes to prevent soil clogging them up. With containers lacking drainage holes, line the bottom with loose coarse material, such as broken clay crocks, pebbles or gravel, to at least one-quarter the depth of the container to drain off water from around plant roots.

The bigger the container, the less watering will be needed. Small pots and containers will generally require watering daily unless situated in part shade. Test for adequate moisture by pinching some soil between your thumb and finger. Moist soil will cling to the fingers.

To help moisture retention, a decorative mulch is useful for container plants, especially those in sunny positions on exposed patio areas. Pine bark, licorice root and coco beans are good for this purpose.

Watering is best done not by overhead sprinkling, but directly to the roots. Foliar feeding is a good fertilizer technique, mixing the granules with water and sprinkling on the foliage.

Shapes of Containers

Round   Cube   Window box

Hexagonal   Cluster   Stepped

Dish   Urn   Cauldron

Barrel   Strawberry barrel   Hanging basket

This container planter features impatiens coleus and variegated vinca.

Window box planter, effectively planted with coleus, wax begonias, dusty miller, variegated vinca and blue petunias

Beautiful specimen of a pot planting of Elfin *impatiens*

Best Display Plants for Outdoor Containers

Name	Type	Flowering Time	Color
Ageratum	annual	summer	blue
Alyssum	annual	summer	white
* Begonia, Tuberous	perennial bulb	summer	all colors
Begonia, Wax	annual	summer	white, red
* Browallia	annual	summer	blue, white
Chrysanthemum	perennial	fall	all colors
* Coleus	annual	summer	red, yellow, orange
Crocus	perennial bulb	spring	yellow, white, blue
Daffodil	perennial bulb	spring	yellow, white
Dahlia	annual	summer	all colors
Dusty Miller	annual	summer	silver
Geranium	perennial	summer	red, white, pink
Hyacinth	perennial bulb	spring	all colors
* Impatiens	annual	summer	red, white, orange bicolors
* Lobelia	annual	summer	red, white, blue
Marigolds, French	annual	summer	red, yellow, orange
* Nasturtiums	annual	summer	red, yellow
Pansies	annual	spring, fall	all colors
* Petunias	annual	summer	all colors
Salvia	annual	summer	red, white, blue
Sempervivums	perennial	evergreen	green
* Thunbergia	annual	summer	orange, white
Tulips	perennial bulb	spring	all colors
* Vinca	annual	summer	white, purple
Zinnia (dwarf)	annual	summer	all colors

* Suitable for hanging basket

Tall American marigold and dwarf coleus make an unusually picturesque combination in a wire container with legs that do not damage grass.

Bright red geraniums and white cascade petunias make a perfect combination in this wooden tub.

Impatiens, wax begonias, coleus, and variegated vinca provide color in these beautifully planted hanging baskets.

Impatiens of all colors in containers, hanging baskets and beds prove the amazing versatility of this tender annual and the reason for its rising popularity.

How to Grow a Hanging Basket

Hanging baskets are an effective way of growing a wide range of plants not only where ground space is limited, but as a complement to many outdoor plantings. A hanging basket for outdoor display can be started indoors several weeks before setting outside after the last expected frost date. This way plants can become established to give early color.

1 — First place the wire basket on top of a large flower pot or bucket to keep it steady while planting.

2 — Line the bottom and sides with a layer of sphagnum moss, moistening it first to make it easier to work with. In the absence of sphagnum moss, a black or green plastic liner punched with drainage holes can be used.

3 — Fill to 1/2 in. of the top with planting soil, using either a readily mixed packaged formula or your own mix, comprising two parts garden top-soil, one part sand or perlite and one part peat moss.

4 — Place plants in position, including a few trailing plants for best effect, such as cascading lobelia and variegated ivy. Water daily, and at monthly intervals feed with a liquid fertilizer.

Buying plants ready-grown in hanging baskets can be expensive, but growing your own from seed is not only a means of saving money, it also enables you to grow a more interesting selection than run-of-the-mill store-bought kinds.

Nasturtiums, for example, will cascade beautifully from a hanging basket, yet you'll rarely find them ready-grown at a garden center, and the flowers will just keep on blooming all season.

Cascading lobelia is another lovely long-lasting subject for hanging basket display, with masses of blue flowers sparkling like sapphires.

Thunbergia — or Black-eyed-Susan vine — is often grown up a trellis, but looks even more exquisite tumbling its yellow and orange flowers with black throats from a hanging basket.

Have you ever seen a hanging basket planted with parsley? Not a flowering subject, but as good to look at as any fresh green fern.

Planting a Hanging Basket

Lovely beds of petunias, nasturtiums and marigolds make a striking contrast to the deep turquoise blue of the swimming pool.

Swimming Pool Gardens

Home swimming pools generally present an outstanding environment for creative planting ideas, particularly in-ground pools where monotonous expanses of concrete paving and chain link fences beg to be decorated with plants. It's amazing how just a few strategically placed annuals will enhance a swimming pool. Quickest color is made possible by imaginative container plantings of sun-loving annuals, especially petunias, geraniums, marigolds, coleus and portulaca.

The long expanses of chain link fencing can be broken up with sun-loving climbers, particularly clematis, roses, morning glories, trumpet creeper and thunbergia. (See chapter on flowering vines.)

Locate beds of day lilies, iris and garden lilies near pools for perennial beauty. Consider tubs of miniature water lilies and bonsai for an elegant touch to sunbathing areas, and beds of smooth stones to break up the monotony of concrete.

The notion that swimming pools should be barren of all flowering plants to discourage bees is a stupid one. After seeing dozens of attractively landscaped pools, I have never been conscious of a bee problem.

Pots of colorful geraniums, petunias and marigolds look delicate next to the stone edging around the pool.

Index